MW01601281

Karachi, After Midnight · Vol. 1, Part II
STORM SEASON
Copyright © 2025 by Khajistan Press
All rights reserved.
Published in the United States by Khajistan Press, New York, NY.
ISBN 978-1-970281-02-6
Writer: Shams Tabrizi (pseudonym)
Editor: Saad Khan

Karachi, After Midnight Volume 1

PART 1   PART 2   PART 3

Counting Traffic   *Storm Season*   *City Electric*
(Jul–Aug 2003)   *(Sep–Oct 2003)*   *(Nov–Dec 2003)*

Editor's Note

I read an online diary when I was thirteen. In the slow dial-up days of the internet in Pakistan, a young gay man in Karachi was posting under a pseudonym: crushes online and in real life, monsoons and power cuts, Urdu poetry, first kisses, family fights, TV shows, and limerence. For six years he wrote. For six years I read.

Life online breaks. Platforms close. Formats fail. URLs die. Paper endures. I saved his posts because they mattered to me. I did not want his voice to vanish. That is why this book exists: to be held, shared, and found again.

The text appears as he wrote it, month by month, with original spelling, grammar, and code-switching. Names, locations, email addresses, URLs, phone numbers, and the writer's original online pseudonym have been redacted to protect privacy. Dates have been uniformly offset. We have added titles for clarity, and a short glossary explains non-English terms and poems he cites.

This is the record of a life: funny, searching, often heartbreaking. Between 2003 and 2009, one gay man in Karachi used the early web to write himself into existence. These three volumes keep him here.

Saad Khan
Founder, Khajistan

Index

***

PART II

Storm Season

Dial-Up Fury

01 Sep 2003
06:38 hrs

seething hatred. abomination and malicious wrath. at my isp. at my windows. at my new pc that got all fucked up. i havent been able to access the internet for some time now. past 3-4 days. i got a new pc. and i needed to install a software for my net to run. but my damned isp didnt reply to my calls or messages so i was without internet then the NEW computer got broke and i had to get it fixed. then when i got that back. the internet wasnt working from the isp. this is the first time i have had to post. i hate the isp and the new computer vendor and windows xp for crashing and forcing me to reinstall it. HATE YOU ALL !!! may you all burn in hell along with characters like adolf hitler and his naughty little mistress ;)

**

Filed under Wrath and tagged: anger, computer, internet

02 Sep 2003

The City That Breathes
19:02 hrs

hmmmmm. after saying that i hate it when i have to live without the internet i will proceed. and for about 4-5 days as well.

large cities like karachi are a world in thier own. their own accents. their own rhythms. their own flavour. and their own city. well i love being a part of this thing. also cities in south asia are generally very volatile and violence prone. maybe due to the harsh weather and the general tension infested life that we lead.

news spreads slowly in the city. rumours spread fast. yesterday two men from a major political party were shot dead in the city. rumours started flying immediately about rioting, arson and generally violence. when i went for a drive today i could see the traffic move faster and more desprately trying to avoid major chorangis(intersection). the first clue to something being wrong. then i heard the news about the two men.

karachi is a city that lives. it breathes. it moves. it awakens and it sleeps. there is complete rhythm to it. and small incidents cause it to become ill like any person may. i love this city. its people. its ways. its colours. its moves. hmmmmm. i think i am being too wierd right now. but that is me. wierd and sensitive.

and in other news. i heard a song yesterday. streets of philadelphia by bruch springstein. a friend of mine in college loved this song. as soon as i heard it severe nostalgia for my college life flooded in. encompassing me. all that was left. was me. the faces of my friends in college. their voices and their words. it is SEVERE nostalgia.

oh what a bitter sweet feeling. nostalgia. it feels so good. but it hurts so bad. nostalgia. ahhhhhhhhh. what beautiful things people go through in their daily lives. nostalgia being one of them. i can still hear that friend of mine laughing and looking at me in that particular signature laugh of his. face slightly tilted. lip slightly curled. eyes half open due to the effect of the song. i will never forgot this. ahhhhhhhhhh nostalgia. what beauty lies in it.

***

Filed under Life, Wrath and tagged: college, internet, karachi, music, nostalgia, urban, violence

02 Sep 2003

After the Riots

23:37 hrs

well it seems that my last post about a little latent tension in the city was right. rumours flying all over the place. karachi saw a lot of violence during the 90s. well thank allah the city is going smooth now. well at least as smooth as most third world cities. but i think i can feel and sense these small currents in the big river.

two shot dead. five shot dead. tension in the city. well i am all too well aware of these patterns. well lets just say that this tension had increased a lot during the day and now is at its peak. lets hope the night will lay it to sleep as it does many other things.

and yes my usual interesting details from my life. i saw a VERY cute guy today. and i stared at him. with no fear or fright. he saw me staring. he didnt do anything. he didnt drag me infront of my parents like i thought he would. he didnt do anything. ahhhhhhhhhh. such a relief.

***

Filed under Lust, Wrath and tagged: 90s, hotties, karachi, rioting, tension, violence

03 Sep 2003

Lassi and Blackouts
15:56 hrs

ahhhhhhh life. what wonders lie in thee. including the delectable lassi that i had 5 mins ago. wow. i love fattening foods that are so utterly wonderful. little glasses full of heaven. ahhhhhhh. life.

 no electricity for about 4 hours today. very windy so wonderful. i called the electrcity department complaint centre about 20 times :) wonderful. from what it seems there are only 3 people there on this number. they were about to loose it with me calling every 10 mins ;) ahhhhhhh. i love teasing the living daylights out of people who pester me.

 oh and yes. my sister was saving her allowance for two weeks. she finally decided to get chocolates from the money and hid them in the fridge. i am SO EVIL. i ate all of em. i love cadburys ;). she told me that she hates me. and that she hopes i will never eat a cadburys dairy milk again. well needless to say. i had kept one dairy milk for her to not be too evil. after her tantrum i ate it infront of her. through the window. AHHHHHHHHHHHHHHHHH. life. what wonders lie in thee.

 and oh yes. whoever was searching for "pakistan dogs" on google and ended up on my site. i am very sorry that you had to go through this. VERY sorry.

and also ... "how you doin!" *WINK*. and just in case someone out there has any misconceptions. i am not a dog.

***

Filed under Gluttony, Wrathand tagged: blackouts, chocolate, food, lassi, prick, sister, stealing

First Night Drive

05 Sep 2003
03:05 hrs

hmmmm. well lets say that life is fine. things are going ok. slow and steady. my cousin persists on smoking like a train. and i persist on trying to stop him. we both stay on our own tracks.

and after that i drove my car from my cousins house to my own. my first car ride. yey. well it was much better than i thought. i didnt kill anyone or destroy my car. well i didnt hit it at all with anything. hmmmm.

well i love to drive. from now on. i will always love it. it is wonderful. but it was nice. more details later.

***

Filed under Avarice and tagged: arguments, car, cousins, driving, smoking

06 Sep 2003

Posts Gone Missing

00:17 hrs

well i wrote two posts both of them effed up. they were good posts. i cant prove it so you will just have to take my word for it. and now i have to go. bye.

***

Filed under Wrath and tagged: anguish, blogging

A Gust and a Song

06 Sep 2003
00:25 hrs

so well i am back. no idea what to blog about. except that i will blog.

as god is my witness i will blog tonight.

i think i should try this. i will type what i feel. as it happens. interesting.

first of all i am very very sleepy and i cant do anything about that. i feel slighltly cold. the wind from the fan to my right is comeing at me in gusts. every gust cold. and after that warm. i like the warmth. the music is playing. slightly loud. the guitars and the drums and and voice are all slightly uncomfortabel due to my sleepiness. my left arm is itching so i will stop typing to scratch it. and oops a drop just dropped onto my shorts. COLD water. very very shocking. the fan is not soundless. there is something in it. there is this sound in it as if something rattling inside it like most ceiling fans. its one special signature of the sound. the pitch and number the frequency. someone called ali just logged into my msn messenger. the sound of the pop up was nice.

subtle yet alarming. barbra streisand is good. nice song. hmmmmmmmmmmmm. i have to go now before i proove to all of you that i am a moron.

***

Filed under Sloth and tagged: blogging, itching, music, sleepy

The Egg War

06 Sep 2003

12:32 hrs

well here i am am. it is 1211 here. i have been awake since 1120. no breakfast nothing. i have only two rupees in my pocket. which can buy me one candy. or two if i get cheap ones that taste aweful. and i am hungry. there is nothing that can barelu resemble uncooked food. i am at my cousins. he is snoring so loud. i think ill put up a sound energy plant and produce enough energy to light gambia and maybe even senegal.

 that said. i am hungry. i love breakfast. i LOVE breakfast. but then again i love lunch and dinner as well. but i love eggs. i have a thing for eggs. it is not only in my mind it has been proven. one day a crooked aunt just to break my pride told me she will make as many eggs as she can and that she will show me that i will stop in the middle of the eggs and not eat as many as i get like i boast.

 it was on! i hated her. she disliked me. we had even spread a few rumours about each other in the past. she had called me feminine. she had actually called me feminine!!! i wasnt gonna take that. i had told someone that she didnt pass college but she failed and tells everyone she has passed. :) people bought it. look i am sorry. but i am evil evil person. even in bed. ;)

so well it was less of a competition and more of a WAR. sortof like the situation in india-pakistan cricket matches. since we arent gonig to fight a war inshallah due to the nukes. and since we dont have cricket matches. so when we do have them it is like do or die. but i digress, more about the whole india-pakistan cricket match scenario later on.

now it is about the "egg war" and the "battle of the breakfast area" as i like to call it. well i wont walk you guys through it but lets say. after 13 eggs. i had won :). she was too tired to make any more. and she was also mindful of the expense she had gone through. so lets just say. crooked aunt 17 – Shams 18. ;) ahhhh the spirit of competition. i am a nice person until someone else starts to compete with me. then i turn into an evil maniac.

i have actually hidden/thrown away a guys toothbrush coz he was trying to cut me off in a conversation. well it is not fair. you try talking and someone cutting you off every 2 minutes. once or twice it is ok. but when you realize that someone is trying to sabotage you you get mad. so did i. well more about my violent competitions later on.

and oh yes. remind me to post about the day when
my pants were ripped ;)
and something beautiful that i read at crash.
I have always imagined that Paradise will be a kind
of library. -Jorge Luis Borges

***

Filed under Envy, Gluttony, Vanity and tagged: breakfast, competition,
cricket, eggs, evil, food, indopak, rumours, sabotage

06 Sep 2003

Ambulance Etiquette

00:54 hrs

hmmm a long day. long long day. but i am very proud today. today when i was in the car. i heard a siren. we didnt understand at first. but then i realized it was an ambulance. usually in pakistan people do not move out of the way for the ambulance. they way we look at it. the guy in the ambulance doesnt have an emergency he just wants to get ahead. yes yes. we are sick sick demented people. i hate this thing with the ambulances. well but today i was very proud. as the ambulance got closer all the cars moved to the left and let it throught. acutally cars moved into the left lane for a long long way so the ambulance sped past. it made me so proud to see this slightly uncommon display of civic sence and human compassion. well i hope whoever was in the ambulance is safe. my love for karachi had increased due to this display. i hope everyone in this city grown to be a model citizen. and pakistan paindabad. well seems like today is my nation worship patriotic attack day ;)

also in other news. today was one of those days that i call candy days. days on which i get to see more than 5 extremely hot guys which would mean guys i would rate more than 7/10. well it happened today.

wow. i am so excited today. well there were ones at the office. at the market. on the roads. everywhere. and one of them was staring back at me. i could feel goosebumps and i could feel a noise like ZUNNNNNNNNNN that is how excited i was that is HOT guy was staring back at me. it could have been anger as well. but i dont care. he was cute. if he wants. he can kick my ass ;)

thats about it for today so ill see you all later on.

***

Filed under Lust, Vanity, Work and tagged: ambulance, civicsociety, emergency, etiquettes, hotties, traffic

06 Sep 2003

Against War   02:02 hrs

the 6th of september was the day in 1965 that india and pakistan went to war. india crossed over the international border between pakistan and india at about 5 am on the night of 6th september and invaded pakistan. pakistan resisted the attack. well the war dragged on for some time. both sides declared a victory and got extrememly excited after the war was over. they still talk about how they whooped each other asses.

 well to india. fuck you. you didnt get anything. you didnt get kashmir. you didnt get any of your objectives. how the hell can you call that a victory. if you dont get your fucking objectives you cant say you have won.

 well to pakistan. fuck you. you didnt capture any indian territory of importance. you didnt get kashmir. you didnt manage to stop india. if you cant fucking get your objectives you cant say you have won.

 to india and pakistan. FUCK YOU! you fucking morons. the people in your countries were in abject poverty during that time. things were worst then than they are now. HOW DARE YOU GO TO WAR !!! nations where people dont get their rights. where people have to sleep hungry and drink unclean water. where the basic necessities of life as defined at that time werent available. HOW DARE YOU GO TO WAR !!! SICK SICK SICK AND PERVERTED !!! damned idiotic politicians and military men. DAMN YOU !!!

 the only thing that we hear about is how many planes were downed. who destroyed whos how many ships. etc etc etc. well noone ever talks about how many people died. indian and pakistani ? dont we fucking count. is this only a game for the fucked up hindu and muslim military personnel to butcher each other and us in the process ? is this how it happens.

 why dont we count ? the citizens and the civilians. we do not want war. we want peace. we want to lead normal lives where there isnt a power cut or load shedding for abotu two hours a day. i want the roads to be built which are currently HORRIBLE in karachi. that is what i want. i dont want pakistan or india to fight wars and kill me. i want them to give me a life which i can lead as a human not an animal like we 1.3 billion humans do right now.

 to india and pakistan and their desire to kill and

maim us only so that they can hide their own political inadequecies. FUCK YOU ! give me clean water. give me continuous electricity. give me a job. give me a working civic system. give me a proper education. give me a clean environment. if you cant do that ... which you havent been able to till now. FUCK YOU !

FUCK Government of Republic of India and Government of Islamic Republic of Pakistan

LONG LIVE PAKISTAN AND INDIA AND THEIR PEOPLE

it is about time the guns went down. and the elements of peace security and prosperity took over.

Long live the people of India Pakistan and Bangladesh.

Pakistan Paindabad ... Jai Hind

South Asia Zindabad.

***

Filed under Wrath and tagged: army, india, indopak, pakistan, patriotism, politics, society, stupidity, war

When PTV Was Art

i saw a drama today. "roohi" casting 'talat hussain'. well lets just say that anyone who can understand urdu. who likes beautiful things. who can appreciate a drama. has to watch it. if you dont watch it you will lose something. you will lose something. watch it. please. i beg of you. watch it.

the acting. oh dear dear lord. the acting. talat hussain and the girl. it is wonderful . the subtle subtle hints. the hints that i can understand as a pakistani. the ghazal being played at a certain point and the wording telling you what is going on. the music being played to heighten or dampen the mood. the way the actors had small ... minute eye movements and worlds of meanings that they held in them.

the subtle subtle things. and the big big meanings. barefoot in the library showing casual as opposed to formal. the way talat is shown and the very very subtle things in which i can see a man who has the morals of a pakistani from a well educated background and who grew up in 1950s and 1960s. oh it is a wonderful drama. you have to watch it. have to.

i am in a wonderous mood right now because of

31

that. it was like i was touched by a ray from heaven. the beauty. the aesthetic. the touch. the feel. the desire. the passion. the 'haya'. the 'hijab'. the aura. the whole feeling of the art of drama touching the epitome of sublime beauty and me watching it. and the ability to share it with someone else, in this case my cousin. it was wonderful. i hope all of you as wonderous evenings as i had today.

pakistan has a very rich tradition of tv dramas. until the late 80s pakistan saw only one tv channel. pakistan television ptv. and they used to show a drama every night between 8 pm and 9 pm. there used to be 4 quarters in a year and 13 episodes in every quarter. there were times when between 8 pm and 9 pm the streets of karachi used to be deserted. throughfares and main roads were emptyish. everyone used to watch the dramas.

and they were excellent. in the script. in the acting. in the directing. in the sets. in the expression. in the settings. everything. they used to be excellent. the art was carried to new heights in pakistan. tv drama. called "drama" lovingly by millions of pakistanis. it was our art. we mastered it. we took it to its zenith. the drama reached its peak in the 80s. tanhaaiyan, waris ... well known pieces of art.

 unfortunately the art of the drama has gone down now. maybe itll resurrect some day later. but by god it was a marvellous time while it lasted. i hope comes back.

***

Filed under Arts and tagged: 80s, acting, art, drama, karachi, pakistan, ptv, sharing, tv, urdu

07 Sep 2003

Ghazals & Mockery

20:21 hrs

i was told that i am a freak 5 mins ago. by my mom. i was listening to my music. usually the problem is that childrean listen to NEW forms of music and parents dont like that. here. i listen to classical forms of music and my mom calls it a cacophony of clamourous sounds. go figure.

well i listen to classical and semi classical south asian music. the raaga. the ghazal. the thumri. the geet. now that the background is done i will proceed.

currently everyone at my home laughs at my music and calls me dead man. lots of eye rolling and messaging about it all the time. that is not it. except for everyone in my house. everyone i know in person laughs at it as well. it seems that my music is so strange that everyone laughs at it. my musical choice has been the topic of many a joke and comment even places where i wasnt present.

well this is ovbviously depressing. i havent come across any one after my university who is nearly my age by about 20 years and shares my musical taste. well i dont know what to say. their loss. a man screaming your loss in the face of 100 % of the other people his age and beloging to his country.

what the FUCK! is wrong with me. why the FUCK

do i listen to classical or semi classical music. when people laugh at it and say who died why are you listening to this. and people have actually started laughing when i told them what i listen to. i mean come on. i think given a choice the social stigma will be more for me due to what i listen than due even to my sexual orientation.

oh he is gay ... too bad ... but he is a nice person.

WHAT !!! he is 22 and he listens to ghazals and raagas ... KEEP AWAY FROM HIM !!! i dont want you mixing with people like that.

i am terribly depressed. i seem to be fond of something that can only be seen as an affliction. it is so horrible and terrifying that people shy away from it. it is so ridiculously funny that people laugh alond at its mention. what the FUCK!!!

i am very very depressed. i cant be gay. now i cant listen to my music. why the hell cant i get even a small break. what the FUCK!!! music DAMNIT it is only MUSIC !!!

***

Filed under Arts and tagged: art, clasiqimausiqi, conformity, ghazal, irritation, music, tastes

08 Sep 2003

Damn You, SquawkBox

21:38 hrs

DAMN YOU SQUAWKBOX! DAMN YOU TO HELL!

they tell me that the commenting is free. now after i use it for some time they say.

" This means that the account owner has not renewed or upgraded their account. SquawkBox Basic/free accounts must be upgraded if they are heavily used over a prolonged period of time. "

this is something that you tell people before they choose to use your software. you have a right to change your rules after i start using your software. but it is sick and unfriendly to the user.

and that brings me to the new issue. i have no idea which software to use now. can someone please suggest it to me.

[REDACTED]@hotmail.com

please help me. and please suggest something that will remain free and not act like a bitch after a little while.

***

Filed under Wrath and tagged: blogging, cheated

08 Sep 2003
Comments Enabled   23:08 hrs

well i have added enetation to my page. so please leave comments on that. i am leaving squawkbox for later times when i can afford it. and also coz it contains your comments.

***

Filed under Life and tagged: blogging

08 Sep 2003

Cockroach Panic   00:28 hrs

well here i am back in my room. thinking and writing as i think. what is the purpose of a government. what is the reason for life to be this way. why did napolean fail from his objectives. what the hell is climbing up my back. AAAAAAAAAAAAAAAA.   AAAAAAAAAAAAAAA. OOOOOOOOOOOOOOOOO.

EEEEEEEEEEEEEEEEEE.

AAAAAAAAAAAAAAAAAA. yes it was a cockroach. and in trying to shake it off i shook it into my shirt. now i NEVER tuck my shirt into my pants. but today about after 4 months i had done that.

so think about the following in a picture.

a man starts screaming. within 5 seconds he is in the living room. running and screaming and trying to hit his back. he does this for 5 seconds. then he starts to frantically pull his shirt out of his pants. still screaming. and then everyone in the house makes a largish circle around him asking. "kya hua ? kya hua?" and then he still screaming takes his shirt off. all in a hurry. and he sees a cockroach run off.

now most normal people would look around sheepishly and put on the shirt. BUT NO!!!!!!!!! Shams had to act like an idiot. so instead of acting like a modest human and wearing clothes he runs after the cockroach. as the tiny creature runs on the gleaming floor Shams jumps on it. he doesnt stamp it. he JUMPS on it.

if you are wondering. now come the WORST part !!! the cockroach died and in such a way. maybe i landed on him too hard. that he obviously burst open.

there was a large cluster of black blobs on an area equal to a large portion of wall in my house. the dead remains of an intruder into my private parts.

also if you are thinking of asking me out ever in the future. i do not do this to 'human' intruders into my private parts. actually they get treatment infinitely better. and now i think i should leave and resume cleaning the wall. YEUCKH ! and let the record show my mom made me do it. i did not want to do that.

***

Filed under Sloth, Wrath and tagged: fear, horror, humour, insects, musings

09 Sep 2003

Ghazal Ecstasy 15:18 hrs

well here i am. i must tell everyone this. anyone interested in listening to ghazals. please listen to "chaand nikle kisi janib teri zebai ka" sung by fareeda khanum. it is wonderful to the extent of being orgasmically esctatic. it is wonderful.

 well today wasnt as interesting as yerterday. but i have noticed one thing. when my computer is working. the electricity is on. and the internet is on. i blog a LOT. i mean i dont notice this but you people who actually have to read all this crap must realize it. LARGE posts full of crap. well what can i do. you are all stuck now.

AHAHHAHAHAHH   !!!!
AAHAHHAAHAHAHHAH   !!!!
MMMMUUUUUUAHAHAHAHAHHAHA !!!!

 and now that my usual hysterics and dramatics are out of the way.

i would like to share a shaer (couplet) with you.

chaand nikle kisi janib teri zebai ka

rang badle kisi soorat shab e tanhai ka

may the moon rise anywhere of your allure

may the colour of this lonely evening change

another shaer (couplet)

daim para hua teray dar par naheen hoon main

khaak aisi zindagi par keh patthar naheen hoon main
i am not lying on your doorstep for ever
what use is this life if i am not that stone
now i will enter the world of the ghazal and leave you all to enjoy what you enjoy.

***

Filed under Sloth and tagged: Fareeda Khanum, Ghazals, music, poetry, urdu

10 Sep 2003

Wind Through the Window   20:58 hrs

well here i am sitting in my room. slightly warm here but bearable. fan on full. wonderful breeze through the window. i love karachi. it is very very windy. that is why i have a continuous wind blowing through my window. and it is always cool and fresh.

sorry to mlc. but i looked on amazon for ghazal cds. and to be honest i didnt find any that someone should use to get introduced to ghazal. most of them are either westernized popish versions of ghazal or ones that i dont think an american would like due their being quite alien. well i will keep on the lookout for something that you might like to have. or i can mail you a cd or something that i will compose myself to show you what i talk about.

***

Filed under Sloth and tagged: Ghazals, karachi, room, weather

Ripped Pants Day

since commenting was down someone sent me 3 email to post this. well here it is.

i should tell you before i proceed. i never pay attention to clothing. i get my clothes cleaned. then i keep wearing them one by one. after wearing one thing for a day or two i throw it in a corner of my room. the clothes collect there. and after a few days (read 2-3 weeks) all my clothes are there except for the 2-3 expensive formal attire that i had. now one day i get up. and i see oh no pants(read lower wear)/shirts(read upper wear) to wear. then i just shove my hand into the pile of clothes. pick out something and wear it. this goes on for about 2-3 weeks more. making sure that the clothes that i wear dont smell while i wear em.

so in this way in about 4-6 i have used up all my clothes and they are all VERY dirty and cannot be worn. then i give them for cleaning which takes about 2-3 days. i sunchronize with the weekend so i kept naked most of the 2-3 days (oh come on ! if you are thinking what i think you are thinking you are perverted). also if during this 2-3 days i have to wear something i had to resort to doing strange things. i acutally once attired myself in a sheet to have lunch.

EVERYONE was staring at me. then there was one time when i wore the a suit to a friends birthday. well lets say i was the only one not wearing a short and a t-shirt and i felt like a freak. but then they asked me to address them. and i made the most vulgar and cheap speech ever to ever fawning crowd of friends.

 this is about the time when i was in college actually about 5-6 months ago. it was a crisp spring morning. a slight chill will you catch if you wear half sleeves (queer sentence structure). it was one of the 2-3 days without clothes. i was looking in my drawer when i saw a pair of pants. i said. YES ! oh oh. but no underwear. what the hell. who needs that anyway. it is just an added encumberment upon me. so i decided to go commando. oh but if i were to know what lay in the future for me.

 well i noticed it too late. it wasnt that cold. my pants were ripped. right at the rumaali (crotch). and it was a slightly biggish hole. and i was like. OH DEAR GOD !!! OH FUCK !!! NO NO NO NO NO !!! NOT YOU !!! ANYTHING ELSE BUT THIS !!! but ahhhhh what childish dreams i had squashed at that instant. no miracles took place. i was as i was.

wearing ripped pants. now i dont wear pants i wear jeans but today was a special day. well i hated it.

i went to class. sat with one leg over the other. wearing pants. a VERY distinguished gentleman i was. sitting in formal clothing in a formal way. oh but if they knew the truth. how shocked would they be. i wasnt distinguished, i was naked. damn it. i was dead scared that day. i didnt walk at all fast all day for fear of hearing a large rip and everything falling apart. and yes i KNOW i wasnt wearing underwear. everyone would have seen my inadequecies. OH COME ON !!! IT WAS A VERY COLD DAY !!! HARDLY A DAY TO GO A PRANCING !!! and that is why i use inadequecies. otherwise you know. i am big. right. come on. i am! come on! i am not lying! ok what ever i shall proceed now.

so the day is going NOT WELL then i go to the cafe. sitting with a group of friends. and suddenly one of them jokes. why are you acting as if your pants are ripped. and we all have a laugh. i probably had a laugh slightly more nervous than the others. my friend realized that. and he said. why are you sitting cross legged. i shot a look at him. he was smiling. he knew !!! HE KNEW !!! damn it ! and he knew i knew. so well he said. HEY EVERYONE LISTEN !!! Shams is not wearting underwear. and they are all like WHOA !!! come on open his legs show us.

oh what nice cherub like kids they were. little did they know that in trying to see the rip they could actually catch big Shams sleeping. (a VERY interesting thing that i noticed as i wrote the last sentence Shams means anger or fury in my language, this dual meaning might get me a few emails from a large number of bottoms out there ;)) well i didnt tell them about me being commando. well i kept quiet. and kept my feet shut as about 8 guys pulled them apart. (come to think of it even this sentence can have dual meanings). well i suddenly told em i am commando. they all said in unison EWWWW !!! and they all stopped. seems like noone wanted to see big Shams.

after that one of the guys jokes about big Shams actually being little Shams. now i never let such an opportunity pass. i always pass some sort of gay comment jokingly and make it seem like i am str8 but just kid about being gay. so i told him he can check out Shams in the bathroom. well lets say

NOONE made any other such comments that day. ;)

and after the cafe incident i came back and changed into nothing again. never again did big Shams get to see the whole university and the cafe himself.

so my advice to all of you. if you cant get caught. and are as intelligent as me. do it someday. commando and ripped pants. and yes this only for one reason so you can post about it. and i can amuse myself as much as you probably have about me. ;)

***

Filed under Life and tagged: clothing, college, embarrasing, exposure, fashion, friends

11 Sep 2003

Blog Housekeeping

14:20 hrs

well i have made a few changes to the blog. the international blogs have been divided into three catagories. now look i dont want to hurt anyone this is a very changeable change. i will push you up if you leave comments. and basically compliment on me a lot ;) if you dont i am sorry.

also i am very busy nowadays so i might not be posting as much as i used to.

and please leave comments on enetation and not on squawkbox.

***

Filed under Uncategorized

11 Sep 2003

September Remembered 22:15 hrs

anyone who reads should read it all. because leaving in the middle might convey a wrong impression.

todays post will be about what happened on the day of 11-09-2001. i was in college back then. had gone for a game of basketball. we can back at around 1900 and decided to get something to eat. i was washing my hands when i heard someone scream. "AA WOO HOO !!!" i was like. "ohkkkkay. seems like people are VERY excited today". then i heard a "YEAH BABAY" i was like i have to hurry up the cleaning and see what is going on. as soon i entered i heard a "this will teach america" again i was like. "what happened ?" there was another "this is what they get for killing innocent muslims" and then there was a "so america thinks they can kill and sit back ... now they arent so safe as well"

now. most of my relatives live in america. and most of them live in greater nyc area. so i was beginning to get worried. just one day ago i had heard of the possiblity of a nuclear meltdown anywhere. so i was worried. i asked one of the VERY excited guys. "what happened? man come on tell me?" and suddenly someone else burst through the doors and said out loud "CNN is saying 10000 dead" i was like "oh fuck!!!" serious sinking feeling. what the fuck is going on. i hope everyone is safe i have to call america". well i thought the guys in my college are idiots.

then a few more excited gusy with news and number. and i forgot about dinner. and i walked dazed to the tv room. yes there it was. a tv. 50 students sitting infront of it. too many. too many. this means some VERY big thing. well i sat down. and i saw the movie of the first tower going down. i saw it. a huge building and it went down in a matter of second. and i saw people jumping out. from what i heard at that time. it was the first time the actual movie was shown. with the movie the level of hilarity in the room dampened and the level of aaaaa oooo whoaaaa s increased. along with a few. "oh my god ... is that a person ?" when i saw the tower go down. i had a huge shock and a sinking feeling. FUCK FUCK FUCK FUCK FUCK. i have a large number of people living in nyc. anyone of them could have been there. anyone. i have to call them.

i ran to the pay phone. there were more than usual people there. they were all talking about it. and they well all calling to get info about america. i called home first and asked them about news. and my dad said. calm down and stay put. do not call anyone in america. let them settle down. they will call you ok. also keep your msn or mirc or email on so we can send you any news. i came back to the tv room. this time. no whalloping. all quiet. people just staring at the screen. with pictures, movies, numbers and things being thrown at us. it was shocking. everyone was quiet. the people who said this will teach america a lesson were thinking about the disaster now.

 10000, 2000, 50000, 8000. i mean come on. this is no small thing. this is so so so big.

 after one news report from cnn we shifted to bbc then someone said lets look at fox. cnn and bcc were shocked. fox was a raving piglet. muslim terrorists. muslim terrorists. muslim terrorist. within 5 mins. everyone in the room was raving mad at fox for their unfounded remarks. cnn and bcc are saying it is too say to say who. fox is saying muslim muslim muslim kill kill kill burn burn burn. we were all shocked. why us ? what did we do? this seems so much like the oklahoma bombing. now americans will beat up muslims all over the country and in the end it will be a group of neo-nazis or aum shinrikio or something.

blaming after evidence is something else. but blaming and finger pointing without evidence. down right wrong. well we changed the channel immediately. now i was also worried about another thing. my relatives are muslims. so if they didnt die in the attacks they might die in the streets. shoot. well i called dad again he said the same thing. all night passed. now after one day. cnn and bcc were ready to say that some evidence was unearthing of there being involvement of muslim groups.

well let me just say that we here in pakistan were as shocked by this as people anywhere else would be.

before i proceed i must say one thing. i am opposed to the killing of civilians by anyone. from which ever side. terrorist groups such as al qaeda, state terrorism such as israel, governments such as the government of burundi. i do not support the killing of civilians at all. even during a war. no matter what. muhammad the prophet of islam has expressly forbidden the killing of anyone who is in bearing arms and fighting in a war. non combattants are not fair game. you cannot kill them period. if they are office workers in the wtc. if they are muslim students an afghanistan madressah. if they are iraqi civilians in baghdad. if they are israeli fishermen. no matter who. it is not allowed. i will not support it at all.

but then america attacked afghanistan. without proof. the usa didnt even have proof at that time. and they attacked afghanistan. with public opinion for muslim blood frothing and flowing. they attacked afghanistan. the media playing its part of making afghanistan seem as the scapegoat. so much so that usa public opinion gave the go ahead. everyone knows that the final piece of proof which the usa cited "as yes now we have proof" was found in a cave in afghanistan after the attack and that too a tape. something that is being forged at the drop of a pin. no really within one day i can get about 100 movies of clinton and bush having sex in karachi. is that proof ? is this fair. if you are in the park and someone hits you. should you go and hit the first person who you have suspicion on ? no i dont think so.

well that happened. we were told of a wonderful future of afghanistan. we were told afghanistan would be a modern democracy. is it ? i dont think so. can any american now say that they have done something good for afghanistan ? any one ? no you cant. coz you havent.

and similarly with iraq. what there. i dont see anything. no smoking guns. no proof. just like afghanistan. just like that. an aggression and then no proof whatsoever. i do not think this is right. it is wrong. you cannot attack other countries to take public attention off the local economy. it is WRONG! anyone who supports the war on iraq should first see the results of the war on afghanistan. if you can say. knowing that you are in the presence of god and your conscience. if you can say that your attack on afghanistan is a success.

there is one thing that i will say. in america the support for attack on iraq was divided half half. in the muslim world it was 97 % against. 2 % dont know. 1% can i get some bread please i need to feed my kids.

there is one thing though. the muslim world could have hated america. but we dont. we know that there are millions of americans who were opposed to it. we know that millions of americans stood up for the rights of iraqis. we know that because we saw it. and that is what unites us. the human sense of compassion for fellow man.

all the citizens of the world united. by the media, by the internet and by every other resource that lets us say. stop it you are hurting me. because the other person will stop. as we have seen. and that is what unites us in the end. all the al qaedas, the neo cons, the kkks, the rsss stand aside. and on the other hand. 90 % of the worlds humans. compassionate and loving. caring and delicate. non violent. non destructive. hostage to the other 10%. yes i am from the 90%. and i am proud of being in that group.

now n few lines from the urdu poet Faiz one of the best poets of the last century.

hum dekhain gay. lazim hay keh hum bhi dekhain gay. jab raaj karey gi khalq e khuda. jo main bhee houn aur tum bhee ho.

we will see. it is imperative that we will see. when gods creation will rule. that which i am and which you are.

the day is not far when decent humans will forge human destiny. not the destiny of one petty nation or another. but the whole of human destiny. with common goals and common feelings. and then will we be free at last. inshallah we will see that day. and then there will be peace and prosperity. at last. at long last.

inshallah.

***

Filed under Uncategorized

Strange Searches

i like to check out on who comes to blog. sometimes people come here through searches on search engines. some of the searches are strange to the extent of being shared. so here is this weeks list of strange searches. i will group the searches according to why i find them amusing.

1 – a very normal casual everyday search. but what the hell is my blog doing in this search.

– pakistan dairy (i like milk, butter, cheese, lassi and other dairy productrs. but that doesnt mean i should be a result of this search)

2 – searches made by people desperately looking for sex. and yes i should feature in these ;)

– karachi slutty girls

– love making in urdu

– msn id of ladies in pakistan

– fucking places in islamabad pakistan

– karachi gay address for meeting

– sex in pakistan

3 – a not so very normal casual everyday search. but my blog in it means there is something wrong with me.

– koi socially depressed (WATCH IT BUD ! there are times that i am depressed but not so much that it should be a result of search queries)

– pakistani khanay(t. pakistani food) (ok i like food and i am slightly fat. but DAMN YOU GOOGLE. DAMN YOU. how dare you pull the good Shams name in the mud here)

– uncommon sence (now this is downright rude and cheap. HOW DARE YOU YAHOO! HOW DARE YOU ? this will be the last straw my involvement in any other search results that drives away possible suitors will cause some serious kick ass)

 oh yes i have go now and irritate the hell out of my mom. i cant understand why she feels irritated when i run muddy hands on her face. oh so till later. ta ta.

***

Filed under Uncategorized

13 Sep 2003
Why We Fear Death
15:31 hrs

hmmmm very bad mood. anger, depression and severe emotional distress. i just wrote a long post. then i deleted it. no need to be a drama queen.

so ill just get excited again. and laugh and cheer like i did in college. i was an idiot back then ;) i used to be the centre of everyones jokes in college. why? because i felt that people bonding over something ... even if it is making fun of me is nice. talk about being an idiotic buffoon. well i have realized that noone on this planet sacrifices any of their own things for anyone else. so that is what i am trying to make myself. inshallah with time i will succeed.

ghalib said that

maut ka aik din muaiyyin hay

the time of death is decided

why cant i sleep all night long

this shaer is playing in my mind again and again. why do we fear death so much when it is not in our hands.

***

Filed under Uncategorized

14 Sep 2003

Romantic Longing

20:50 hrs

I dont know why but I am in a VERY romantic mood right now. Listening to my romantic music. Old indian songs. "saagar kinare". Old pakistani songs. "akelay na jaana". English songs. "clapton – layla" "elvis – the wonder of you". Oh god i am in a VERY romantic mood.

I am feeling a deep deep longing for someone or something. I cannot explain what this desire, this urge is for. I really can not. It eludes me. But there is a very strong desire for something. I get this feeling on and off. Specially after watching a movie that I loved very much and wanted to continue. Sometimes on a beautiful evening with a light breeze and cloudy skies. Sometimes in summer nights when the fan is on full and I havent had any human contact for some time and I am listening to music.

I cannot be sure but it is a desire for love. A desire to love someone. A desire to be loved by someone. The love that you have for a partner, a spouse a lover. That love. A relationship. To have someone in my bed. And have him there even when I am awake. To have afternoon tea with him. To watch uncountable sunrises and sunsets with him. Allah ! how beautiful a world you have made.

 Ending on the note that if any of you get any cheeky ideas pertaining to my situation, do share them with me ;)

***

16 Sep 2003

Birthday War

02:59 hrs

well i didnt post yesterday. sorry. birthday ;) and well i like birthdays very much. i get to be rude and mean and noone minds :) muahhahaha. i had a pact with my mom and sisters before the birthday that i will be rude and mean and they have to bear with it. they did bear with it.

but at 12 tonight they all came into my room. and guess what. they are my family after all. threw LOTS of old glue on the floor. and to add to it. they threw some oil as well. since it isnt my birthday i have to work as well. which means i just got finished with cleaning my rooms floor.

lets just say. IT IS WAR !!!

***

16 Sep 2003

The Big Rip

16:52 hrs

hmmm. well it was a normal day until i got off the car. when i got off the car my shirt got stuck in the door and i heard an audible rip. hmmmm. what the hell. but when i looked at my shirt i couldnt see it. feeling slightly strange i told my cousin about it. he said maybe a small rip with a big noise. so a started to move away. after two or three steps there was a gust of wind.

WHOOOOOOOOOOO !!! WOWOWOWOEEEE !!! my pants were ripped at the crotch. BIG RIP ! felt like i was naked and all that wind in my pants. well unlike last time (entry on 2003 09 10) this time i was wearing underwear. only the rip was HUGE. i mean i asked my cousin if he could see it. and yes he could see it when i was walking. WOW! BIG RIP!

needless to say i didnt care if anyone peeked inside. their perversion not mine. so like our plan we went out and had lunch. i kept my legs closed. oops. embarrasing. but nothing happened. i walked back to the car. VERY slow lest any more rips. and here i am blogging about one of the more embarrasing days of my life. ;)

***

Filed under Uncategorized

17 Sep 2003

Neem Tree & Ten Points
20:44 hrs

in other news. i just got a "neem" tree for the garden and my grandfather who loves gardening put it in the ground. so its been one day. i am keeping my fingers crossed. i love the neem tree. it is tall. it is leafy. it is green. and it seems like one helluva tree. so i want it to grow. wish me luck.

also in other news i am chatting with this guy for some time. and i seem to think that i like him. also i think he reads my blog. so i shouldnt be saying this over here. but whatever. he is nice. and shockingly he watches the same tv programs i do. which is such a coincidence and i am very excited about this. so lets see how that proceeds. and he even has a nice name (no i am not the most unreasobale person ever ... i think it counts what a guys name is)

in still other news. yesterday was allahs present to me on my birthday. well i saw so many beautiful beings i was out of control.

i rate men from 0-10. since i dont usually talk to them this is a completely physical rating. i saw a guy who i rated 10. which is VERY uncommon. since the last one was about two years ago. and then i saw two guys who i rated 8. now lemme tell you that is no ordinary day. i was so happy yesterday.

the 10 pointer i saw when i was out with my cousin and friends for tea. he sat on the table infront of mine. and i could see him well. WOW! 10 points. that is equal to david fumero not a lean feat. well i dont know why but this line from a coulet kept going on and on in my head. it is in farsi but it is very pertinent.

ae turk e ghamzazan kay muqabil nasheesta

sitting in front of the ballad singing turk

here turk means beautiful man

well that happened yesterday. WOW nice.

***

Filed under Uncategorized

17 Sep 2003

Hottie Revelation

23:20 hrs

i VERY interesting thing i heard today. from an old school friend who i met online after a very long time. she told me that girls in school (10 grade) used to like me a lot. and shockingly i was considered a hottie (?????) well i have no idea where they got that from. in school i always thought of myself as a loser kinda guy. shy/feminine/horrible at sports. but i was a fun guy to be with. you know the people magnet. funny and excited and cool. so now i have no idea what to think. maybe i was cool. wow. that is interesting to find out.

 i wont even begin to tell you guys what this did for my self esteem. also how much i want to lose weight and get in shape now.

***

Filed under Uncategorized

19 Sep 2003

Eight Out of Ten
01:15 hrs

another story about my life. a little while ago i met this guy on mirc. well i liked him immediately. and we chatted a bit. then he told me he was str8. i said DAMNIT!

well we became friends. chat a lot even today. and today he asked me what i would rate him. i said 8/10. he was very happy. then he said why i never mentioned him on this blog. so here is a mention of him. his name is "sirus".

so sirus are you happy now that i mentioned you ;)

also i think i should say this. 8 is VERY uncommon. and VERY high in the rating.

***

Filed under Uncategorized

19 Sep 2003
The Talk
13:50 hrs

DAMN IT!

horrible day today. had THE talk with my mom.

well she just told me to get of pc. when i started to whine she said NO come here now. so i went to talk to her.

***

19 Sep 2003

Denials & Straight-Acting 22:35 hrs

OH MY GOD !!!

This blog presents the worst picture of me. I want to make this clear. I always write in my blog when I am emotionally active. So it might seem that I am a VERY emotional guy. Which I am not. I am a normal guy. Only Allah knows what that is.

Well I have decided to handle the Mom/Gay thing with denials and acting straight. So wish me luck.

***

Filed under Uncategorized

20 Sep 2003

00:09 hrs

Falling for T

WOW WOW WOW !!!

Well I was chatting with the guy I told you all about. T. And OH MY GOD! He is very interested in Urban Planning. I am fascinated by the subject. What are the chances ? I mean come on.

Over the past two days I have chatted with him about. South Asian History, Architecture, Music, Society, Arts, Culture. And again OH MY GOD!!! OH MY GOD !!! I have completely fallen for him. He is interested in everything I am interested in.

I mean I cannot say how VERY uncommon it is. He is interested in South Asian Classical Music. He is interested in South Asian History. He is even VERY good in Urdu but his English is shaky. BUT OH MY GOD !!! He knows French. This is SO cool. So wish me luck. Please dear God dont let him read this.

Shams over and out.

***

Filed under Uncategorized

On Time & Civilizations

21 Sep 2003
00:01 hrs

Life goes on. Day by day. Month by month. Year by year. Century by century. Millennium by millennium. People live people die. Feet walk the streets and are no more. Cities rise and cities fall. Civilization prosper and then become mere tribes. Time consumes all. Nothing is left. Save two things. Wonders for which manking toiled in the blistering sun and the freezing cold. Names of men great and tall who rise above the crowd.

Looking from an external and outside perspective. We are so so small. One Man does not matter. Neither does one villiage or city. Or for that matter nation or civilization. They are all transient details. What matters in the global movement. The global movement for excellence and perfection. The global movement of ideas, thought and ideals. The will to learn and the will to strive. That is what remains. All else is lost.

Makes me seem so small. Make my problems so petty and unimportant. The bigger picture. The real bigger picture. To think how Man developed from the wild tribes 7000 years ago to this level today. Within 7000 years we have found out how to split the atom and hence destroy ourselves. But we have also made the UNO to save us from that. We have made weapons but not books. It is time that man matured and acted as the real inhertor of the 7000 of history. It is about time all war ended.

***

Filed under Uncategorized

23 Sep 2003

Engineer Beggar

00:20 hrs

Have not been posting for some time. The reason can be seen from the following story.

Me, my cousin and a friend went for tea. We were sitting in the tea shop. Just ordered. My cousin had just lighted his cigarette. We had ordered three "doodh patti" (extra milky tea). Suddenly I saw there was someone standing right besides me. I looked up. There was a man standing there. The waiter who was passing by told us he needed money. We were confused.

He suddely started speaking. I usually avoid such encounters because generally people who beg arent worthy of the money and I dont want to say no. But this was no general case. My cousin suddenly something that caught my ears. I cant understand English to him. I looked up. The guy was looking at me and started talking in English. "I am a Mechanical Enigneer. I have been in the Army. I dont have a job. I have to feed a family". Although heavily accented, but, grammatically correct English. I was shocked.

Only educated people know English in Pakistan. A mere 3 % of the most educated people can talk the way he did. I was shocked. Is Pakistan really gone to this level of poverty, destitution and social destruction. Has it come to this that people with a bachelors degree in engineering, not the liberal arts, engineering have to go begging for tea and a biscuit or a little money. I mean what is this coming to.

While he was asking for money he broke down and started sobbing. Every sob hit on my nerves like a hammer. Every sniff was an explosion in my thought. I have no idea how I sat there. I have no idea how i got the audacity to ask my cousin if I should give him money. I have no idea how I could have possibly sat there and been so cold and steely.

Well we gave him some money. Came back home. I was quiet in the tea house and on the way back home. The others didnt even stop for that. But as soon as we were home. There was a lot of merrymaking.

That is how we feel about this. Surrounded by abject poverty and destitution we have become used to it and do not even pay it heed for more than 15 minutes. But one thing is going on. For the last 2 days I have been hearing a poem written by faiz and sung by iqbal bano in my head.

Hum Dekhain Gay

…

Sab Taaj Uchalay Jaen Gay

Sab Takht Giraey Jaen Gay

…

Bas Naam Rahey Ga Allah Ka

Aur Raaj Karey Gi Khalq e Khuda

Jo Main Bhi Hoon Aur Tum Bhi Ho

…

 We will see

Imperative that we will see

…

All the crowns will fall

All the thornes will fall

…

Only Allahs name will remain

All Allahs beings will rule

That I am and that you are

…

 Let up hope and pray for the best.

***

Filed under Uncategorized

24 Sep 2003

Architecture & Urdu

12:45 hrs

first of all i will give you all some unsolicited advice keeping in mind that what happened to me yesterday can happen to anyone. never stand under a tree with LOTS of birds. you might get your clothes dirty. and also you might have to go home to clean up. and later on find out from other people that you missed a perfectly excellent evening.

something very interesting happened last night. i was chatting with the guy (whome i have been chatting with every night for some time now :)) and he asked me if i have a fetish about uniforms and i said. yes. then he asked me if i have a fetish about guys in (his profession here) and i said yes. he was VERY amused. then i asked him if he had a fetish about guys in (my profession here) and he said yes. well come on it did seem interesting at that time.

also he asked me to meet him. sure i know him for some time now. but i have never met someone i met over the internet. also i have never been on a date. so i am dead scared. i think ill stall and stall and stall until some time. then i will meet him. shivers running down my spine. but the thing is we have VERY VERY similar interests. there are four things that we are both VERY interested in and i dont think there are people interested in even one of them. this is what makes this so interesting. architecture, urban/town planning, south asian history and south asian classical music. i mean come on. what are the chances. i cant believe this. he is nice and educated. and also. he knows french;) his urdu is impeccable. what more can i ask for. and yes. he has a sense of houmor. he actually has a sense of humour !!!

 oh wait. ill be back in 5 mins. i think i am going to faint with delight ... ... i am back. ok bye
:)

***

24 Sep 2003

Lost Email, Found Friend
12:56 hrs

the guy who sent the email where he said that he was surprised to see allah and gay in the same sentence. please email me again. i am a moron and i deleted the items of my inbox after i finished reading your email. you seem like a person one can be friends with. please dont leave me alone because i am an idiot.

***

Filed under Uncategorized

Brother, Not Boyfriend

24 Sep 2003

14:23 hrs

i went to get my sister from her school today. she is in the 6th grade. i went inside to pick her up. she and her friends were giggling together like girls for 6th grade do. very interesting. as soon as i got close enough she smiled and gave me her bag.

 when i came outside she told me all her friends were asking her about who i am. so i asked her what did you tell them. she told me that she didnt tell her friends that i was her brother. taken aback i asked her why ? she said because i didnt look good enough and i wasnt wearing proper clothes. she was right. loolz.

 i have never felt this rejected in my life. and since you all know i dont even have an iota of self respect. it didnt even make me feel bad. so that fact that i dont feel bad is what is irking me right now.

***

Filed under Uncategorized

26 Sep 2003

Lunch Date Anxiety
11:48 hrs

when you chat with someone for everynight for two weeks. it is a general expectation that you meet. that is what happened here. T was asking to meet but not mentioning it. it was like a question suspended in mid air and i knew it was there. well yesterday i felt the urge to take the next step and meet him.

i told him about it and he was quite happy about it. so we decided to meet. since he is slighly bus we will meet friday for lunch. i know i know what kind of a horrible date is a lunch date. but see i dont call it a date i call it a meeting. and T noticed this word VERY much "meeting?" isnt that a date and i was like "yeah yeah". so basically since it is lunch which is like a TERRIBLE date so we are having a meeting. god i hate this. i think he felt bad coz i called it a meeting and not a date. but i think ill make it upto him later on ;)

so well we both do not offer friday prayers. :) so we are going to meet on friday. and yes one horrible thing. we havent decided. hmmmmmmm. seems like i will have to talk to a lot of friends to find out where we can have decent lunch in karachi. :) so all of you. wish me luck on my date ... err ... meeting thing :)

and how are your lives proceeding.

also i read recently that the french revolution took place not because the french were the most wretched but because they were the best off. hmmm.

***

27 Sep 2003

Tonight's Playlist   04:13 hrs

i couldnt make it today. i meet T every night at 2300 on msn messenger. but today i couldnt. i got late. i came home at 0230. DARN. i miss him. and i have nothing else to blog about. so i will just type the songs that i listen to tongiht as i sorf the net.

Nazia Hassan – Camera Camera

Iqbal Bano – Muhabbat Karney Walay Kam Na Hon Gay

Jefferson Starship – Its not over till its over

U2 – Montgomerys Visit

Vivaldi – Winter

Engelbert – Love me like i love you

Fareeda Khanum – Chand Nikle Kisi Janib Teri Zebai Ka

Jagjit Singh – Zulmat Kade main meray

Scatman – Scatmans world

Mehdi Hasan – Pyar Bhare Do Sharmeelay Nain

Rolling Stones – It must be hell

Rafi – Khoya Khoya Chand

Indian Oldie – Saagar Kinare

a huge mixture of indian and pakistani movie music. along with south asian classical and semi classical music. and european classical music. and the new western music.

ill go now and let you listen to your own musics. ;)

***

27 Sep 2003

Nazia & Green Pastures

04:23 hrs

and as soon as i finished the last post i heard a song by nazia hassan.

she was a wonderful singer. i think she was the first to introduce popular (pop) music into pakistan at a larger scale and level. her songs are evergreen. every pakistani in my age group will remember her songs like childhood memories ...

sooraj chalta hay ...... aap jaisa koi ...... zara chehra to ...... dhere dhere ...... ooee ooee :) ...... sun meray mehboob sun

and so many others. these are songs that if you start to sing with someone in my age group they will start at it for no reason at all. it is a common cultural bond between pakistanis of my age. nazia hasan and her music. the many many super hits of our childhood. the songs that we heard over and over all over the media and on countless cassette players all over pakistan.

nazia hasan was a pakistani cultural icon. it is so unfortunate that she is with us no more. and it is so unfortunate that she died so very far away from her land.

may allah make pakistan good enough for pakistanis especially those who want to live here but are forced by circumstances to leave pakistan for greener pastures in the west.

***

Filed under Uncategorized

27 Sep 2003

The Unfilial Son

12:15 hrs

well needless to say i having HORRIBLE problems adjusting to family life after college. i know i know everyone in pakistan lives like this. but i cant. its done. i cant. its horrible ok. you dont know. it is horrible.

they are always expecting things from me which i cannot give. i mean come on i am not a prophet or god. they want me to be this and that and to do this and that. i cant do all that. i got used to an independent life after college. i cant do it.

and since i cannot come upto their expectation which i think i should. i feel like a loser and a failure as a son and a brother. damnit. i hate all this. i actually feel like i am failing all of them. i feel like i am not coming upto any of my responsibilites.

yes you are right. i did have a fight with my mom today as well. but today she won. she told me that i should be living alone coz i am a liability and not an asset. she told me that i am not at all street smart and even her daughters are better at guy things. then she told me that i have only hurt her and never been a source of comfort to her.

blah blah blah. long story short and my own interpretation. she wished she had some other person for a son. GOOD!

***

01 Oct 2003

Nothing to Report

11:28 hrs

i havent been posting a lot lately because nothing much is going on. i havent chatted with T properly for about 3 days now. sometimes hes busy sometimes i am. but we leave each other many many mails to tell each other sorry i couldnt come.

work is boring.

home life is boring. no fights. just everyone very cheerful and getting along like nice people. UGH. boring.

what else. well nothing else. life is going along. boring.

i will post if anything interesting comes up or something.

hmmmmmmmm. well i think it is time i left and read the posts of other bloggers who do lead interesting lives. ;)

***

Filed under Uncategorized

Date on the Horizon

it seems that my life is finally interesting. i have something to blog about. not just something. four somethings.

 i went to a gym yesterday. and then today. well lets say my body above the navel is a big sore of pain. it seems like all of my muscles were pulled at by nimble yet deft fingers of persian carpet weaving girls. i cannot raise my hands upto my face. i cannot open my arms wide. i canNOT stand my sister punching me in the back. i sure hope this pays off :)

 i went to pick up my sister from her school again. this time i went dressed and early. at the prescribed time the school bell rung. children ran out of their classes like a swarm of locusts from the sahara spying the irrigated agricultural exapanse of pakistan. i mean it was a stampede. but this time my sister didnt feel down because of me. but the whole episode reminded me of the time when i was a kid and used to RUN out of the door as soon as the bell rang. as if i stayed for one minute the sky will fall upon me and not kill me but make me incapacitated for life.

 i had a normal 1.5 hour chat with T. it is final i am going to meet him on friday. my first meeting ever. i used the word 'date'. he noticed it. but it seems he was very happy to see me use this word. seems like i am the one stalling and not the one rushing. but he is very patient. and oh yes he told me he likes edward said, noam chomsky and iqbal ahmed as modern philosophers. i LOVE him.

and the last point is that PTV is doing an all night transmission on music. the guest on the show is 'tina sani'. the show is about music. and it is a WONDERFUL program. so anyone from pakistan who can catch it. CATCH IT! they have shows songs/ghazals by mehdi hassan, nazia zohaib and many others. tina ji herself sung a song LIVE completely live. so i am off to watch the show. WATCH IT.

***

Filed under Uncategorized

03 Oct 2003

Date Tomorrow   01:41 hrs

OH MY GOD! DATE TOMORROW ! AA WOO HOO!

***

03 Oct 2003

Citizen, Not Student

02:19 hrs

something that i was thinking about. finally was able to phrase it properly. being a pakistani and seeing pakistan and all its facets. and seeing life in karachi as a citizen and not a student.

 woe onto him who lives at the gottedammerung of his civlization. more woe onto him who remains a human during that time and has all the human feelings. i cannot explain how much sorrow i feel now for all such people in the past in the present and in the future.

***

Filed under Uncategorized

03 Oct 2003
Engine Failure
14:14 hrs

FUCK FUCK FUCK FUCK FUCK! I hate my fucking luck.

Today WAS the big date. T came back from Islamabad and mailed me that I can come for lunch. In comes my fucking luck.

My car broke down. So I thought this will be over soon. No need to cancel the date. So I went to the mechanics shop. He said the engine is DEAD. It is DEAD. And I thought WHOA that is not good.

I had to cancel the date. I have to get the engine made. Which is VERY expensive. Damn it. I hate my fucking luck.

To top it all I have been going very slow with T. He has hinted at this but he is VERY patient and understanding. And now he is going to think that this is just an excuse. I mean come on. Engine failure. VERY VERY VERY uncommon. Damn it. I will have to talk to him now. I hate my fucking luck.

***

Filed under Uncategorized

03 Oct 2003

Sexy American Accent

16:51 hrs

OH MY GOD ! I hate sitting in a mechanics shop when he just takes the cars engine apart. One small and significant piece by one small significant piece. I mean come on. It is very irritating but you still have to do this. It is like working a night time guard at an empty museum. Noone is going to come in. But you still have to be there. Futile.

I did not mention this earlier. But I talked to T for the first time today on telephone. And he has the most sexy voice ;) Although his accent is a VERY thick American accent. Which is something I will have to work on. But for now I am only going to wallow in the fact that the guy that I am going to meet has a VERY sexy voice.

***

Filed under Uncategorized

04 Oct 2003

Airport of Accents

11:28 hrs

i went to the US in the summer of 2000. it was interesting. the scenery for the last hour as we approached new york from europe was WONDERFUL. then we landed. it was a LONG LONG LONG horribly long flight. 8 hours from karachi to manchester and 7 more to new york. i was ready to sleep on the COLD marbel floor.

 when i landed i was hungry, tired, weak, nauseated, dead and basically VERY VERY crappy. my sister was the same. since i was a guy i was supposed to act normal. making all this SO much more harder. and well i have to admit. i was SO completely turned on by american guys who are quite HOT.

 we had to wait for one hour before our luggage arrived. apparently there was something in someones stuff and they had to check everything. well it wasnt so bad. one hour. not such a big deal. after that we went to immigration. now this is the FUNNY part. something on the form wasnt clear. OK. my english is perfect. althought that doesnt show on the blog because i dont pay that much attention when i write it. but come on. 700 in SAT means good english (continuing after the OBVIOUS self praise and aggrandizement) so it really was unclear on the form.

there was a lady there. i asked her excuse me can you help me. from the look on her face i thought she couldnt understand. so i said excuse me again. now. out comes a voice. a HEAVY nyc accent. one that i couldnt understand at that time. honestly i couldnt understand her. she said something. now i was blank i heard sounds but no english words. and she must be thinking. oh great one of those i dont know english undereducated morons from third world banana republics. so i thought hey who not do this. i started speaking in a british accent. and from here on she also started speaking in 'her' british accent. we spoke for 10 minutes and only got across one thing. what to write on that one line on the form.

at that moment across the atlantic. 1 million britishers of a strong linguistic background and excellent accents were turning in their graves and wishing to god to pull them up away from me and that woman.

so my answer to Crash ... you americans have VERY VERY heavy accents as well. the only people who do not have accents are indians and pakistanis. ours is the truest form of english. we have the largest english speaking community in the world and hence we decide what proper english is ;) match that ... huh ... and all of you brits out there ... cheerio chum you shouldnt have ruled us if you didnt want this to happen. now we have your language ;)

***

04 Oct 2003

Day of Rampage

15:13 hrs

i am extremely saddened as i type. karachi has descended into chaos and violence.

i have seen two burnt busses. one burnt truck. one burnt oil carrying container. one petrol station broken up. five burning tyres in the middle of roads.

my cousin wanted to go for pizza. we went out in the car. and we are here after 15 minutes too scared to go ahead. some people got killed yesterday. today is the day of the mob rampages. it is the day when we commit suicide as a nation every few weeks.

the traffic in karachi suddenly changes if there is something wrong. cars and busses move at a different frenzied pace. they move on different roads. the amount of traffic changes. that is what happened today.

there was a heavy police presence. there was a heavy parmilitary presence. i saw three fire trucks and two ambulances today. more than i have seen in the last few months. allah help us all and keep us in his protection. it is saddening how we behave as a nation.

when we were going along for the pizza we decided to go ahead even if there was a like trouble ... but then we suddenly saw two towers of smoke up ahead after the bridge. we didnt cross the bridge we came back.

i am at my cousins right now. the worst of the situation is near my home. i am very worried. one of my sisters is at college. the other has gone for classes. i am scared ok. they are gonna come back home. allah only knows how they will get back home. this is scary damn it.

this happens every few months in karachi. i sudden breakdown into chaos and violence. why must we do this. why must we have to endure this life. it is not fair. why must we feel this way ever so often. it is not fair. i can only pray that our lives improve with education and understanding and we are finally able to lead productive lives.

may allah keep us in his protection and mercy.

***

Filed under Uncategorized

Stones & Sirens

04 Oct 2003
15:22 hrs

oh yes ... another fire engine. yarrrrr. this is not good. i feel the pain of my people. those who are closeted into their houses right now out of fear. those who are running away from the roads to be safe. those who are trying to keep the peace by using their batons. those who are burning the cars and tyres out of rage. i feel pain for all of this. this slow self inflicitng of wounds upon our nations body and soul. this slow death and destruction. i can only wish and pray for this to end. oh damn. another fire engine.

i cannot explain this in a single word in english ... mobs throwing stones indescriminately as all cars passing by ... burning cars, buses and trucks ... breaking up petrol stations ... shopekeepers closing their shops out of fear of arson ... people trying to avoid the troubled areas ... but there is a single word in urdu that will make the exacly situation exactly known to the listener "hangaamay".

may allah keep us in his protection.

***

Filed under Uncategorized

Crows at 6AM

It is about 0601 on a sunday. I have no ide.
work up one hour ago. Just couldnt sleep. May.
because of the slightly hot weather and also because
I slept early tonight. Something in the
neighbourhood of midnight.

Well here I am up at 0603 on a Sunday morning. It
is awfully quiet out there. No noises in the house. No
noises from outside. Except from the sudden yet
interesting sound from a bird or a crow or and eagle
or a parrot or any other natural flying object.

I was just looking at a few blogs and I realized that I
am a part of a community. Like a real community I
read peoples blogs. Who read my blog. We all share
our thought and emotions. And most of all we have
gotten connected in a way that we have become
friends in a way. Only with the internet at our hands
could this have happened.

Oh God. I hate the sound of Crows. It is an UGLY,
low droning croak. Hate it.

I like to collect satellite images of places. I love
watching the world from far off. But close enough to
see what is there. Cities and towns. Rivers and
dams. Deserts and oases. It is really nice. For
starters I would recommend. Specially for

Americans. Terraserver. And also my all time favourite.Visibleearth, NASA

***

Fields & Hunger

05 Oct 2003
16:24 hrs

Kyun Damaktey Huay Shehron Ki Farawan Makhlooq
Hasein Khaet Phata Parta Hay Joban Jin Ka
Kyun In Main Aaj Sirf Bhook Uga Karti Hay
Why do the citizens of glowing cities
Life only for the desire of death
Beautiful fields of overflowing crops
Have only hunger growing in them
May Allah give us the chance to become human beings.
Pakistan Paindabad

***

Filed under Uncategorized

Only Local Fires

06 Oct 2003
18:43 hrs

Hmmmm I think I should clear this out. It is not that extremely bad. The thing is it was only local violence in an area of the city. Unfortunately it was in my area of the city. It is really not that bad. Calm down.

***

Filed under Uncategorized

Hate You, Yahoo

06 Oct 2003

18:54 hrs

OK. I have gotten used to strange searches. But whoever out there searched for "free desolate island sex pics" on Yahoo. WHY?

I mean come on.

And Yahoo. I hate you. How dare you add my link to such ghastly searches.

And I have learnt NOT to say sex or any other strange word on my blog again.

***

Filed under Uncategorized

07 Oct 2003

Set to PKT   12:46 hrs

Finally fixed the time to Pakistan time. Lets see if it works this time.

***

Filed under Uncategorized

07 Oct 2003
One Hour Ahead
12:50 hrs

I have finally been able to successfully shift to Pakistan Standard Time on my blog. Only it is one hour ahead of the real time. But whatever. One hour ahead of real time is much better than 12 hours ahead of the real time.

***

07 Oct 2003

Blog Refresh
12:52 hrs

I knwo I know a lot of other people also made changes to their blogs. That is why I finally decided to update mine. So how is it ? Comments ?

***

Filed under Uncategorized

08 Oct 2003

Learn Before You Judge

00:39 hrs

No idea what to type. Except. Please learn something about Homosexuality before you pass your judgements. It is NOT a choice. It is NOT a liking. It is NOT an inclination. It is an orientation. People do not BECOME gay. They ARE gay. I think we should all try to learn at least as much before we pass judgements. And as far as religion in concerned. I do not think I can believe in a religion that says Homosexuality is unnatural. Because I am a Homosexual and I am natural. What other proof do i need of that religion being completely farce.

 Waisay I have noticed that I at times write things on my blog that according to Pakistani law will be counted in blasphemy and I can easily be given the death sentence for my blasphemous opinions and thoughts ;). So basically. Pakistani Legal System – FUCK YOU! Pakistani Mentality of Fucked up Religious Extremism – FUCK YOU!

***

08 Oct 2003

Witness to a Body

19:17 hrs

Well I am shocked today. SHOCKED. I came out of my house about 1400 today and someone told me that there is a dead body at the end of our street. I tried to go there but there was a HUGE crowd there already. About 50 people. Then I was told that the body had been sent to a nearby hospital. I came back. Into my street I saw a trail of blood. Leading to a Rickshaw. And the seats of the Rickshaw were blooded. I was shocked. Later on when the Police came again into the neighbourhood. They said they think that maybe the passenger tried to rob the Rickshaw owner. Who resisted and got his throat slit. FUCK! Well eye witnesses said that the Rickshaw owner walked about 100 feet to the nearest road with his throat slit and blood gushing out of his wounds. His clothes drenched in blood. God. It is horrible. The suspect has not been caught. I saw the blood twice today. It was very very depressing. There is this guy. Who probably had a family to feed and people to take care of and now he is dead. So damned depressing. One life lost so uselessly. I only hope that he went to a place better than he left.

***

Filed under Uncategorized

When Anger Rules

08 Oct 2003
20:27 hrs

This is what happens every fucking time. Whenever I am in a fight or in a tense situation I do this. Everytime.

Damn it. I never storm out. I never go for a walk. I never stop talking to the other person. I never do something that might make them feel sorry. Instead I punish myself and try to make it seem as if everything is ok. NOT for my sake. But for the other persons sake I dont fucking want them to feel bad.

And every fucking time. EVERY fucking time I end up hurting both me and the other person. What the Fuck should I do now? Haan ? What?

I take care not to hurt someone. And they get hurt all the same. What the fuck do I do ? If I dont care they will get hurt all the same ? WHY ?

Damn it. I dont know what to do. It just sux. Why is that everytime I stand at a fork both the choices given to me lead to a situation worse than I am alread in. So I get a choice. And the feeling of helplessness when I fail. I fucking hate this.

I had a thing with my cousin. I didnt talk to him after that. Now I cant storm out of the house. Coz then he would think that I am very angry. And I cant stay in the house coz then he would think that I am

there to mock him. See. I hate this. Two choices
BOTH FUCKING SUCK! DAMN IT!

***

Filed under Uncategorized

08 Oct 2003

Lost July Archives

21:01 hrs

Why can I not see my archives for the month of July when http://[REDACTED].html is an actual webpage with my blog on it. Why ? Why must all this happen to me.

And while I am lamenting the problems of my blogging system. Squawkbox – FUCK YOU!.

If anyone out there knows how to solve the problem with the archives. Please tell me.

***

Filed under Uncategorized

09 Oct 2003

Net-Boyfriend

10:03 hrs

I chatted with T again last night. It was wonderful. I am really beginning to feel this developing into something meaningful. I mean I have nothing to compare this with. But it feels right. We have been chatting for a month or so now. And I have started to feel restless at 2300 everynight because that is when he comes online. He has also made it clear that there is something from his side as well.

Last night was wonderful. After three days when I saw his nick pop up in my MSN messenger I felt so happy. Well we talked and talked and talked. Yes I know it might seem boring. But talking isnt all we are going to do when we meet face to face.;). Well I asked him if I can use his name on my blog. He said no. So I am still going to use T. Also I thought I should take a step and ask him something which made me feel slightly queasy. I asked him if I can call him my boyfriend on the blog. And I waited for the answer. And shockingly he was so happy about it. Now it is confirmed. I am the one who wants to go slow. Hmmmmmmm. Then he suggested that since we havent met I should call him my net-boyfriend. Which I think is very cute.

I HAVE A NET-BOYFRIEND !!!

And then the really good news. I am going on a date on Saturday night. :). I mean a date. Since that is what we both called it. This is very very nice. My first date. And it is with someone who I like a lot for a first date. It is with someone who I can talk to easily since we have so many common interests. It is with someone who likes me too. I am really looking forward to it.

I HAVE A DATE ON SATURDAY NIGHT !!!

AA WOO HOO !!!

I think it is VERY early to say this but. I think I am somewhat in love. :). I know I am not a 16 year old school girl. But this is how I feel. I feel like I am slightly in love. Thank god I never fall in love all of a sudden. These things take their time with me. So in about a few months ill be in love. ;) WOOHOO!!!

Oh and yes. DAMN IT! He forced the address of my blog out of me. So lets just say that the blog is being written on yellow alert and I reserve the right to not say everything on the blog. Although todays post was clear (White). From now on there is a code. Red = Severely Censored. Orange – Mildly Censored. Yellow – Slightly Censored. White – Not Censored.

***

Filed under Uncategorized

Dreaming the Taj

09 Oct 2003
14:53 hrs

I am thiking of adding one thing to my blog from now on. Yes I know you have seen it. A picture of me. That noone can recognize in real life. So I wont lose my safety cover. Ill keep changing the pictures from time to time. So do tell me that I look cute and remember that I have not shaved in some time.

Along with my pictures I will be sharing pictures of buildings. Preferably ones whose architectures I admire.

This time it is the Taj Mahal in Agra. It was built by the fifth Mughal emperor Shah Jahan (Khurram), the Qaisar-e-Hind at that time. His empire was the largest producer of manufactured products and goods in the world at that time. The Taj Mahal was finished in 1653 AD. It was made by the Emperor in memory of his beloved wife Empress Mumtaz Mahal (Arjumand Begum). The Taj Mahal is the considered the epitome of the Indo-Muslim architectural tradition.

And it is a building that I would love to visit and see one day.

***

Filed under Uncategorized

Loose Talk & Histories

I just saw a comedy tv show. "Loose Talk", starring 'Anwer Maqsood' and 'Moin Akhter'. Two very seasoned comedians. I would consider all of those unfortunate who can understand Urdu and belong to the South Asian culture but havent experienced any of the many programs that these two have done together. The episode I just saw was about a poet. And from now on I will make it a point to not miss "Loose Talk". There was a point when I laughed so hard that I had a coughing fit. I always say that the duo's shows should be seen on some media where we can pause it. Because it is very common to get into fits of laughter so long that you miss ensuing jokes.

 I am thinking of adding an online poll to my blog as well. I think ill put that on tomorrow.

 I saw a documentary on Discovery on Sinan the renouned Turkish/Ottoman architect from the time of Sultan Suleiman the Great. It was wonderful and the clips of the Suleimaniye mosque were exquisite.

Another interesting thing I came across. Homosexuality was called the Persian or Turkish Vice in Europe until recent times. Due to the prevalence of it in Muslim countries. It is also said that until very recently the only places that did accept homosexuality to some extent were the Muslim countries in the world. And to think that today these very nations are the most oppressive about being gay.

***

12 Oct 2003

The First Date

11:25 hrs

I went on a date yesterday. I will give a description of it and answer any obvious questions along the way.

It was my first date ever(Ans. No I am not a freak). It was interesting, wonderful and thought provoking(Ans. I know! the strangest adjectives).

T and I met outside the restuarant where we were supposed to eat. :). He was the second to enter. It was nice seeing him all of a sudden. He looked much better than his photo betrayed. We said our his and hellos. Then we went and got seated inside. He seemes slightly nervous. I was probably so nervous that I could not think straight(Ans. straight, pun unintended). I think was quite nervous which I remained throughout the evening. Although I loosened up later on but I was nervous even when I was walking back.

T suggested the nights fare. It turned out to be very nice. We had a nice long conversation ... about everything. We talked about our past, Pakistan, Government Officers and so many things. It was more like meeting with someone I know than a first date. That is why I really enjoyed it. I was thinking that there might be nothing to talk about. There might be LONG uncomfortable periods of silence(Ans. No neither of us is dull). But I was wrong. There were no glitches.

We decided to get dessert some place else. So we left. This is where the date becomes a one of a kind and the only of its kind. I had to go to a bathroom(Ans. NO! I am NOT a cat) Well I had to go. I wasnt feeling well maybe something I ate. Well I told him this. We went to a place. Their bathroom was out of order. So the poor guy took me to another place where I went to the batroom(Ans. No No it was not the freakiest date ever).

After that we went for dessert. As soon as we entered the shop I felt a waft of a wonderful aroma. I thought it was chocolate but T told me it is more of waffles than of chocolate. Well another interesting time. Ice creme. A lot to talk about. Mainly politics I think. And I finally managed to look at him while he talked to me. He looked visibly nervous. And I was thinking "Damn, if he is nervous then I should be freaking out right now." But then I thought that it is maybe his cute little way of being. I am talking VERY cute here. ;)

Well we left that place. Then we went for a drive. A

long long drive along Karachi's roads at late night. We had chatted about this on MSN before and we both knew we loved it. So we went. Oh and yes it was his car all along. We went to the sea coast, Saddar, Shara e Faisal and Clifton (Ans. Not in that order) and it was a wonderful drive. I kept yawning all the time(Ans. No I am not an idiot). He told me it is contagious and he started yawning as well. So I blame myself. Well it was a wonderful drive. Talking to him. The scenery. I thought it was very romantic.

 Since it was the first date I didnt know what to do or not to do. I think I might have told him that I am not going to have sex on my first date ever. I think he told me that he didnt even ask me at all and it is OK. I think I was VERY VERY emabarrased by this question. In this paragraph I have said I think whereas I actually did do this and I remember it vividly I just do not want to accept it because that would be horribly embarrasing(Ans. NO I AM NOT AN IDIOT stop calling me one).

 Then he said he will drop me off. So we started off for my place. He took me to Shara e Faisal road. Because we both love it at night. We kept going and talking. Going and talking going and talking.

Suddenly he says. Shit. I say what. He says I was supposed to turn a LONG LONG time ago. I said OH I thought we were going for a drive(Ans. read ahead I am coming to it). And he said I have to drop you off and I had to turn. I asked him why he overshot. He told me he thought I was going to the airport. And I was thinking "YES, he is like me, he is human, he makes mistakes". Well we had a HUGE fit of laughter on the fact. He told me he has been going to the airport so much that he was going automatically. So I thought wow. STRANGE DATE. Looking for a bathroom then going to the airport(Ans. yeah yeah you snicker I bet you never had a date with so much happening).

 Well the rest of the journey was uneventful. When I was about to get out of the car I forgot all of my manners. And I was going to leave but he said it was a wonderful night(Ans. Yes. I forgot to thank him or comment on the date). But as soon as he said this I told him it was nice. He told me I was cute. I got so excited I mumbled something. :) I do not remember what. And that was the end of the date. I was supposed to meet him later on MSN but my internet just got up 15 mins ago. So. Here I am.

Oh and yes. We stood in front of the sea for about 10 minutes. With our back to the Karachi coast. We looked out towards the sea. Random lights from ships coming to the harbour. The starts. The inky blackness of the water. It was wonderful. I love the beach of the whole Karachi coast line. I had always thought I would go there on a first date. And we did. It was very interesting.

All in all it was a wonderful date.

**

12 Oct 2003

Night of Shab-e-Barat

11:41 hrs

Last night was the night of Shab e Barat. It is a muslim holy night where we pray all night and we visit the graves of out departed. It is as much a part of our culture as it is of our religion. I went to the graveyard last night. There were SO many people there due to Shab e Barat. With Rose petals and water to sprinkle of the graves. Also with Agarbattis and Candles to light on the graves. I could smell the rose petals and Agarbattis from a good half kilometer away from the graveyard.

There is no system of graves so it is VERY VERY much like slum of graves. Here and there high and low. Finding the graves of loved ones is hard. You have to remember markers such as trees, rooms and BIG graves. Well we found the grave of my grandmother. But we could not find that of out grandfather. Althought we looked a LOT for it. But alas this is the way things happen.

There were many many people hobbling along. On the thin linings of the graves. Looking for graves of their. It was interesting to look at. There were many many beggers over there. It was more of a surreal experience the graveyard. The candles and the smell of the agarbattis and rose petals. All those people in islamic hats. All those beggers praying loudly or wailing for money. It was a very moving experience.

I think the idea behing going to graves is dual. First is to realize that we too will die one day. This life is not for ever. So we should take care of this life and lead it in the best possible manner. Second it is to see the graves of people. And feel the ensuing feeling of "I didnt do enough for him/her" which at least I always feel when I see their graves. This will make us feel that we should cherish and love all of those who are with us and treat them in the best possible way.

I will say that going to that graveyard last night was a wonderful experience I wish you all had a chance to do that as well.

***

Filed under Uncategorized

12 Oct 2003

Pictures, Not Faces
13:54 hrs

I have finally put up the pictures page. There is a death penalty on Homosexuality and Blasphemy in Pakistan and I cannot reveal myself as I am VERY guilty on both counts. So youll have to make do with these pictures. Have fun.

***

Filed under Uncategorized

14 Oct 2003
Mystic Rhythms
02:05 hrs

I was listening to Abida Parveens songs today. I realized that there is a complete tradition of this devotional / mellow / mystical music in Pakistan. Including Qawwalis and Ghazals and other musical forms. They all have a similar flow of rhythm. A slow and steady increase. That is supposed to coincide with the growing level of 'Wajd'(Trance) that the listener encounters. Well I always get a strange feeling when I sway my head like the mystics do at Mazars and Mosques to such songs. It is slightly surreal. Well I am going to get a collection of such songs and have a session of a few hours. I dont know what it will lead to but I think I have to try.

 I have seen that India (read south asia) is a land of spirituality. Yoga, Music, Rituals and the feel of the land and the people. It all allows for a lot of spirituality. I am from this land and I have been fed this culture and civilization slowly all my life. And I feel it. I think I am going to try and find out this side of myself.

 I also this that capitalism is not the perfect system that Uncle Tom shows it to be. It is very dehumanizing. It deals with robots and not humans. It is despiritualizing. It doesnt deal with the reality that humans have a soul and a body and that you cannot give them money and luxuries and expect them to prosper. You have to have a purpose, happiness and many other things that only money cannot provide. It is about time we devised a new system for yourselves before we are too far gone into the abyss of capitalism and forget the right path.

I havent been able to chat with T since our date. I miss him. :(. Well inshallah tomorrow we will have a chat. And I think it is so cute. :). He has started to comment on the blog. And T I like it when you comment. Also, yes you got the spelling of my real name correct. Which is a rare rare feat. :).

***

Filed under Uncategorized

Small Joys, Big Goodbyes

15 Oct 2003
01:41 hrs

All day today internet services all over Pakistan were disrupted. It took me about 45 minutes to get this post into my blog today.

 I forgot to blog about yesterdays event. Here are the details. Last night I had to go to the farewell ceremony of my manjhali (middle of three) sisters academy. If people tell each other at least 50 times that it is the most horrible night ever then you should belive them. I left after a little while as it was excruciatingly painful. People single handedly murdered the concept of music. People destroyed all remaining vestiges of humour. The entire philosophy of dancing and its implementation were ruthlessly mauled that night. It was the death of culture and civilization as we know it.

 I was thinking about tea shops today. Since I went there three times today with my friends. Groups of friends usually love hanging out on tea shops in Pakistan. There we can have Chai (Tea) or Doodh Patti (Milky Tea) or Sabz Chai (Green Tea) or any of the many other forms of tea. A biscuit or a paratha. Basically it is something that is a part of our daily lives. It is a small and subtle addition to the bank of things that make our lives so beautiful and worthy of living. We should enjoy each and every of these small things in our lives to the fullest.

Oh and yes. California. Good Job. Now at least we know that democracy doesnt always work. Thank god we Pakistanis do not have to bear the burden of being the only fools on this planet.

***

Filed under Uncategorized

Non-Violence & Pomegranate   02:31 hrs

I havent been able to chat with T since our date. I hate this. I miss talking to him and I havent been able to. When I get up tomorrow I will kill the owner of my ISP. Then I will call T and try to see how he is. Although his many emails have told me he is fine. He thinks I am avoiding him. Which I would SO not do right now :). But more about that tomorrow.

Today I went with my friends to the fresh fruit juice shop. Where we sit on small rickety benches. Drink a LOT of milk shakes and talk about stupid and boring (not got straight guys) things like girls and women. Since it is on a major road I just look at the men passing by and pass the time. Today I had some Pomegranate Juice. WOW! I would suggest all of you to not pass up an opportunity to have fresh Pomegranate juice.

Today while crossing a road I saw an accident. As it is the norm in Karachi both the drivers got out promptly. Now people usually talk for about 30 seconds before they lose it and fists fly. An education adds 30 seconds to this total. Age adds about 30 more. Beards reduce 30. Well this time it started about even before 30 seconds. I know, WOW! My friends and me had to go over. Literally pull the two apart. Then I felt depressed all night thinking about where Pakistan is going to. What are we, Dogs? Well the thing is even if you beat the other guy into a hospital he is NOT going to give you money for repairs. WHY IN HELLS NAME are you fighting then? It is NO use at all. Except to keep up your over inflated egos which should not even exist because you are animal enough to get into that fight in the first place.

I am completely against all forms, formats and kinds of violence. I believe in non-violence.

Oh and yes I have made a change to the Blog. Now Pictures is a like to my Fotolog. I think the pictures would be available there if they arent just leave a comment so I can try to do something.

***

Filed under Uncategorized

17 Oct 2003

Read More, Feel More   03:42 hrs

Still not able to chat with T. This sux. I hate this.

 I met a college friend today. We had fun and I got a much needed exposure to someone from my college(NO! I am not wierd). Finally. We watched a part of a movie and we laughed at the same jokes(NO! I wasnt faking it) something that happened for the first time since I left college.

 I finally saw a collection of books that made me realize that I need to read a lot. Why? Well because I like to read. Not so that I can act pedantic and intellectual and show other people down. No! come on. You have to trust me. I like to read because of the experience. Not because of the effects.

 Damn it. I knew I shouldnt have said that. Now you all know my little secret.

 In other news. I listened to this Ghazal by Farida Khanum "Chaand Nikle Kisi Janib Teri Zebai Ka". Since I had three orgasmic spasms of pleasure during the enterprise I cannot but tell you enough the NEED to listen to it.

***

Filed under Uncategorized

18 Oct 2003
05:08 hrs

Live and Let Live

I had the most amazing omelette this morning. I love eggs and sometimes when you like something and you are VERY hungry you can have WONDERFULLY edifying experiences. Like this morning.

I came out to a straight friend through the blog. Gave him the address. Let him find out the rest by reading it. He took it amazingly well.

Had a long long discussion with him. It also included a discussion about the concept behind Religion in general and Islam in particular. Why do people with a religion start to stop thinking and start believing? Why must religion be steeped in dogma and OLD OLD traditions that what we do not need in our day and age? Why must more importance be paid to actions / prayers as opposed to the intentions that those actions / prayers are based upon? God I am a VERY VERY irritating athiest for mose people who believe in religions.

Ok I might even say that I am ok with other people following their beliefs. But damn it do not judge me or force your opinions on me just because I am an athiest. And specially because I am in a minority wherever I live. you do what you want. And ill do what I want. Jio Aur Jeenay Do (Live and let live)

***

19 Oct 2003

Mother Wars   01:09 hrs

Well this is a long boring post about the problems that I am facing as of this moment. I would suggest most of you to not read it and spare yourself. Those who continue CANNOT blame me.

We I have been having severe problems with my mom. We fight all the time. All the time. It is horrible. She isnt like this with anyone else. I am not like this with anyone else. We get into fights on small things and I we cannot stop and end up completely emotionally exhausted and irritated with each other. I never got along will with my mom. Never. Not for the past 5-6 years that I remember well I have NOT gotten along with her at all. We do not agree on ANYTHING. Last year we checked out around 40 houses and we did not agree on ONE of them. The ones she liked I did not the ones I liked she did not. Except for food we are the opposites in EVERYTHING. I mean it is intersting meeting someone like that but you can not live with someone like that. We would always get into fights. Our likes and dislikes are completely different and we cannot stand each other choices in anything. If she wasnt my mother and we had to live together one of us would be dead by now. Humans can not put up with this.

 Well to top this all off she is also having trouble due to PMS. So she is horrible to all the men in her life. I am a guy I cannot go around all day talking about how I feel and think and continuously sharing my emotions with her. I AM A FUCKING GUY OK !! GIVE ME A FUCKING BREAK !! I AM NOT A PIG !! BUT I WILL NOT GO ALL DAY SHARING MY EMOTIONS !! So I am not a good son. I am a failure as a son as I do not compliment enough and I do not ask enough. So she thinks I do not care. And she in continuously angry at me. For the last two weeks every time we meet we get into a fight within 2 minutes. It is like the ending phases of a long and very very bad break up. It is horrible. I cannot stand her for 1 minute. She cannot stand me for one minute. Well so I had another fight today with her. I got so angry I left home. I am at a cyber cafe outside my house. And basically I have left home.

 Well everything aside I am in a state of shock. I am a complete failure. I can not get along with my mother. I am such a complete failure. What kind of an animal am I? This is the worse thing that can happen to a Pakistani. I have been taught about the importance of family all my life. And I believe in it as well. But I completely fucked that up and I cannot make amends at all. I fucked it up. I fucked up the most beautiful thing in my life. I am such a complete failure. I have hurt them all my leaving them and I have hurt them all by being horrible with them.

***

Filed under Uncategorized

19 Oct 2003

A Prayer for Futures 01:12 hrs

I know I do not have the right to do this. But,

Prayer: Please Allah may every new born baby in Pakistan that will be gay die at birth and not go through what our society puts us through.

***

Filed under Uncategorized

Let Me Cry

19 Oct 2003
01:19 hrs

And to think that I have always kept my familys happiness and feelings above mine. It would seem strangely ironic that I end up hurting them so much. Which also shows me how good I am in my life. I am a fucking PIG. I hate my life. I curse the moment I was born only to hurt my parents in return.

I feel like such a complete disgrace and a failure as far as my emotional and mental capabilities are concerned. I ran away from home. I mean that means I am very very emotionally and mentally unstable. I cannot get along with people. I cannot keep up a normal decent relationship and even that with my mom fro crying out loud. What the hell is wrong with me. What kind of a moronic buffon cannot even get along with his mother and then fights with her all the time an runs away from home. Someone in college said that I am not emotionally stable and I think he was right. I am unstable. I am a freak. I am a lunatic. I feel like shit right now.

And yes. Fuck me. I cannot even cry. I FUCKING want to cry. But I FUCKJING cant. Maybe God's way of getting back at me. Why dont you believe in me. I am an egotist if you do not do what I say I will make your life hell. WELL I BELIEVE IN YOU!!!

OK !!!! IS THAT WHAT YOU FUCKINGH WANTED !!!! WELL HERE IT IS !!! —— LA ILAHA ILLALLAH! —— SEE I READ THE KALIMA AND I AM A MUSLIM NOW!!! SO STOP TORTURING ME !! At least let me fucking cry.

***

Curse, Café, Confession

I talked to a few of my friends from college. I asked them all if they think that I am a horrible, rude and mean person. They said no. I asked them if I was like that at all. They said no. Well I wasnt a horrible person. But now I am. My sisters say that I am a horrible person. I went to hostels. They say that people become strange after going to hostels like me. They all think that I was always this horrible as I am being to them. I am not like that. This is only because of my relation with my mom. I do not want my sisters to grow up in such an atmosphere of tension. I dont want them to have a completely horrible childhood because I was an asshole. I dont want to fuck up my sisters life as mine already is. I hate this.

 I would curse the day I was born. I would curse the fact that I am such a complete failure and a disappointment. I would curse that fact that I was engineered by God to hurt others a task that I seem to perform so well. I would curse being gay. Yes I would curse being gay because it has given me so much hurt. So fuckign much hurt. Life is not worth this. I would choose death over life if only there werent all these other lives linked to mine. I curse the fact that once we are born we cannot leave without hurting so many other. I curse the fact that I am a curse on my family.

I hate this. Here I am sitting in a cyber cafe. My family probably worried about me. That I left in a fight. And I am here. My one action has made me a complete failure and a complete loser in one moment. All in my life that was worth anythign was lost the moment I walked out of the door. I left it all. I left my house and I lost it all. Now I can neve sleep without remorse. But at that moment I was so angry. Her being the same person that she was. That irritaing tone that angry voice that she talks to me always with and never with motherly love. Always angry at me.

Well if you are always angry at someone. For even as long as two weeks it meand only one thing. You hate them. Yes my mother hates me. Not because of her. Because of me. I am worthy of her hatred. No mother would hate her child. I must have pushed her to this state.

***

Filed under Uncategorized

19 Oct 2003

Turn It Down

01:41 hrs

See I cannot get along with her for many reasons. We do not see eye to eye on anything. We can NEVER watch the same channel on tv. Because she watches Indian TV which I hate and I watch oldies which she hates. I cannot listen to my music as she thinks that I am supposed to listen to YOUNG tunes. Rock and Pop and Metal sortof dance techno hip hop unbeat stuff. WHAT THE FUCK IS THAT! I never want I GET SO FUCKING IRRITATED when someone questions my music. LISTEN TO YOUR DAMNED MUSIC. LEAD YOUR OWN FUCKING LIFE AND LEAVE ME ALONE.

GIVE ME MY FUCKING SPACE! LEAVE ME THE FUCK ALONE! PLEASE! PLEASE! PLEASE! IN AM NOT IN A ZOO LET ME HAVE A FUCKING MODICUM OF PRIVACY! GROW THE FUCK UP AND LEARN A FUCKING THING ABOUT HOW TO FUCKING LIVE! DO NOT FUCKING STIFLE ME!

I mean they interfere in everything. What I wear everyone comments on it. What I listen to EVERYONE comments on it. I spend an exorbitant amount of time on the net. Granted. But everyone comments on that. What I eat everyone comments on that. I cannot live like this. People are supposed to behave themselves and not judge someone ALL THE FUCKING TIME.

***

Filed under Uncategorized

19 Oct 2003

Dust & Curtains

01:54 hrs

I want a normal house. Ok we shifted a few months ago. Everything is not perfect. So we need to make a few changes. Ok. there is construction OK. But I want the house clean. There is dust everyfuckingwhere and on everyfuckingthing. DUST! DUST! DUST! Why the hell cant they leave the house clean. WHY the FUCK is it so FUCKING DUSTY. That is not the point. The point is that when I say it is dusty my mom says no there is no dust. I just completely fuicking burn up on this. completely fucking burn u up. Then I walk to ther nearest wooden furniture and swipe it (sghit i cant tyope peroperly) with my finger to show her the dust. Then she says well that is natural. I mean come on DUST. FUCKING DUST! She just completely fucking denies it. DENIES IT!!!! LIES TO MY FUCKING FACE !!!! just burns me the fuck up. I cannot stand dust. Then I am told on my face that there isnt any. I cannot live like that.

There is a concept of 'Purdah' in Pakistan. Even though I was an athiest before this post I think the purdah is a social obligation. So I asked the women in my family to put up curtains because when they dont people can see inside the house. Anyone can see inside the house from the street. And they never closed it. NEVER. I used to fight with them all the time and they didnt agree. They used to do that same funckgin thing here are well. Tey jsut use dt o say(i cannot even type rignt now ... ill atak e a break then ill tyeep) they say nono ... the curtains are drawn. Then I show them the open curtains. They are like oh sorry. SO WHAT AM I ? DO I SEEM LIKE A FUCKING LIAR! They never never never close the curtains properly. Now I am ready to promise that for the last one week everytime I look at those curtains they are always open.

THIS HAPPENS EVERY TIME. The food isnt good. Oh no it is. My bathroom doesnt have a strong enough gjet of water. No it does. The chicked isnt tender. Yes it is. The curtains arent closed. Yes they are. There is dust on the furniture. No there isnt. My bathroom isnt properly cleaned. Yes it is. My rooms floor isnt properly cleaned. Yes it is. WHAT THE FUCK!!!!!!!!!!!!!!!!!!!! I saw it and I commented. I am not a fucking liar. Why the hell wont you just listen to me. I cannot get along with someone who does this. Whenever I say someting they deny it without even checking. I hate this. I cannot get along like this. It drives me mad and I dont know what to do.

Look I can do this myself as well. But then they shouldnt say. We pay so and so to do this. Then dont fucking pay her. Tell me to do all this and I will do all this. But dont lie on my face and dont call me a liar.

***

Filed under Uncategorized

19 Oct 2003
Say Thank You
01:03 hrs

And what is with the cooking. Well she cooks. I love her food. Then she wants me to thank her. She wants me to say that I appreciate that she cooks the food. And she wants me to say thank you. I know it is a reasonanable thing to ask. But what the hell. I am the man of the house. If there is a noise at night. I have to check that out. I have to check out things security wise. I have to check out that there is noone prowling at night. I have to decide to use the other door and other window so noone will think about gonig in.

 I do my share of things but I do nto go around asking people to thank me. I do not flaunt what I do for my family. I am just not like that. And I dont want to deal with someone who is. I never said thank you because frankly when my mom said say thnk you to me. I thought of how much of a horrible person she is (which she wasnt I agree) and I never said thank you. I cannot stand it. Why should I. If she considers me family and if she sees that I do stuff too that she doesnt appreciate.

  HOW DARE SHE ASK ME TO SAY THANK YOU!!! HOW DARE SHE !!! what the hell am I. A guest. An animal. WHAT ? I do stuff to noone ever thanked me for that. WHY THE FUCK SHOULD I. Well we had a few fights on a few days due to this. And I stopped eating at home. Well now it isnt that much of an issue. But she still sometimes tells me to say thank you but I dont. Beacuse it is unfair. And I will not. I know I am being unreasonable but I cannot help it.

***

Filed under Uncategorized

19 Oct 2003

No Privacy at Home

02:12 hrs

She does not have any respect for my privacy. A little while back I got two letters. She opened up both of them. WHAT THE FUCK! MOM! GET A FUCKING EDUCATION! WHERE DID YOU GROW UP ???? IN A BARN ? I had a huge fight with her about this. Then she snooped around in my closet. She actually looked at private stuff that I put in there because I had no idea someone would be looking inside my closet. If it was my sister who is about 11 then it is ok because she is YOUNG. But my MOM. What kind of a person would do that. She still routinely checks on my things. And I fight with her. She will not stop. She thinks it is her right.

 Then she conitnuously keeps moving my things. All the time she keeps moving things from my room outside and things inside. Everytime I leave the house and the room. She changes something. She moves furniture in and out. She moves my stuff in and out. Without asking me. She just moves things. Sometimes I work hard in arranging things but she doesnt givves a fucking rabbits foot. She just moves things because she wants to make it harder for me. And I have had a fight with her every time and she NEVER listens. She always does that.

Now you tell me. If you have a huge fight with someone over something. You get very very angry that you punch the wall with all your might. And you tell them not to touch your stuff. And even if she does then nto move it too far away. But she enever listens. What does it mean. It means she doesnt care. SHE JUST DOESNT FUCKING CARE! SHE WANTS TO HURT ME! That is the only way I can see it. There is no oterh possible explanation.

Can she really be so seriously boorish that she doesnt know what privacy is and that you are not supposed to move other peoples things arbitrarily. Or does she do this due to some reason. I sure as fuck cannot decide. What doo you think >?

***

Filed under Uncategorized

19 Oct 2003

Left Home at 2AM   02:14 hrs

This is one of the worst nights of my life. I have left home and I am in a cyber cafe that smells bad.

**

19 Oct 2003

Talking Like Adults   02:19 hrs

Well I know these are issues that you have to deal with. But it is hard ok. Hard to deal with the same thing day in and day out. The same thing. It becomes stifling and kills people slowly. I would have loved to deal with these problems. But I cannot talk to my mother. Due to college I am used to talking to rational people.

I tell and issue. You think about it. You reply. Then I listen to you. I think about it. Then I reply.

SHOCKIGLY I couldnt do this with my mom. She doesnt listen to me at first. Then I get irritated and I start to disrespect her and to talk in a completely unacceptably uncultured way(I know I am wrong and I am sorry about it) but I cannot help it. Then she starts getting all judgemental and the talk goes to fuck in hell. We cannot talk because I cannot get the idea across which she might want to listen to.

At times she says the most absurdaly shocking things. Well once when I was criticising her. Yes I agree I shouldnt but I cannot stop It is what I am it is what I am like and I dont do it a lot just oon two or three things that I really hold close. Well she went so far as to say that someone has had some magic done on me so that I start hating my family. this will

BEVER DO. I cannot talk to someone who will blame everything on magic.

This happened today as well. As soon as I entered the house she scowled and behaved in the most aggressive, hateful, vengeful and angry way just like she has been for the last 2 weeks. I am human too I responded. And she said that the house in Manhoos – Bad Luck. And that as soon as I enter into it it changes. I cannot talk to someone who is like this. I mean come on. Why wont you ever think of what is wrong with you.

See how she shifts the blame. I have been accused to being under a spell too hate my family. I cannot talk to them. They FUCKINGSTAERT TO TALK ABOUT MAGHCI. How am I supposed to get my ideas across to them. I can not. I can not talk to her. SHe will never listen to me rather she will think I am under a spelll and blame that. So no problems will ever get solved.

***

19 Oct 2003

Tears in the Dark

02:33 hrs

I am ctying now. I am dfukckgn criyng. I am crying alike a fuckinggirl.

***

Filed under Uncategorized

19 Oct 2003

The Weight of Being an Only Son

03:08 hrs

My mother knows I am gay. Which is hoorrible. Because Pakistanis in that generation can not be open to the idea. They cannot be ready to accept or live with that. Because they never saw it. So they dont accept it at all. Well I am an only son which is a very very lucrative position on society. So it gets worse. I am an only son and I am gay. I havve no idea how she is dealing with this.

 I dont want to hurt my parents. But they will be. They will be hurt that her only son is gay. I am sure that when I was born and maybe even before that they would have thought about me. Fantasized about the life of their son. They would have thought of my family and my wife and how they will get along perfectly with her. How they will have grandchildren. How I will have a perfect life. They would have fantasized and thought about this so so much. The family and its progress. But well I cannot do that. They will be shattered. I dont know how I will ever tell them that their can not come true. That they will have to see thier lives turn into futile exercises.

   My father and my mother. They are both reasonably religious and I dont have any idea how they will take it. How they will feel. What they will think. I cannot tell anyone else. As my abnormality will cause the family honour to be wiped out. The 'izzat' or honour of my 'khaandan' or family will be finished. Noone will marry my sisters. Noone will respect my father or mother. Something they deserve because of their honest lives and their hard work on raising their cildren. This will be a devastating blow to my parents. It is well understood that honour and dignity are more important than everything. Death with honour is preferred without question to life without it. I have idea how I will pull my family into this.

***

Filed under Uncategorized

Morning After Revelation

Well it is the morning after. I spent the night at a friends house. I got up early and left. I do not want to pull other people into the vortex that my life has become.

Well I am going home now. I talked to a very good friend of mine about the whole situation. He made me realize that these problems are not due to anything else but the fact that my mom knows that I am gay. I am sure it must be very hard for her to bear. I cannot blame her. So well I am going to have to come out to her. Since my cousin was already forced into telling her that I am gay I think I should do it as well. And stop her from both hurting and be scared.

I hope things work out. I just hope I do not hurt her very much. I mean come on. Only son ... gay. WHOOSH! It is like shattering all her dreams and taking away everything that she might have fantasized about for the last 20 or so years. I do not want to do that. But then again it is her fault for snooping and forcing people to tell her the truth. She violated my privace now she will get hurt. I can not do anything about it.

In a country like Pakistan. Belonging to a muslim

middle class family. I have no idea how to come out to my mother. This is not the west where people come out every day and there is a whole concept behind this. This my dear is Pakistan. And I belong to muslim middle class family. What do I tell them. That I am interested in men. My mom never even teased me about girls in my life except for when I was very young.

We are very very frank with each other in my home but this is too much. Anything relation to relationships like these are not discussed. How the hell am I supposed to talk to her. What will I say. I have no idea. I will have an idea later on. But now I dont.

So wish me luck that I do not kill my mother with this horrible news. It is one horrible thing to tell ones parents. I can now imagine what so many people go throught when they have to come out to their parents. I hope she takes it will. I know she will not.

***

The Coming Out

I went home. As soon as I saw my mom. I told her. WE HAVE TO TALK. NOW! So she came with me to room. And I told her.

I dont think I 'came out' correctly. I dont think I did it at all correctly.

She said. What? I bathed you when you were young. How can you be gay. I said ammi I am. She said but you normal physically how can you be gay. I said ammi I am normal physically and I am gay. So you like men and you are normal physically? I said yes ammi. It is not a physical disorder. She said. Oh ok!

She accepted that and we went on

Well at first when I talked to her she thought I was made into this by someone. She kept asking me. Is is due to your friend XYZ in school. Is it due to your friend ABC in college. Is it that guy you used to go to gym with when you were in the 11th grade. I told her NO NO NO. She didnt believe me. It took me half an hour to convince her that noone made me gay. That I was always gay.

She didnt believe that but we went on.

She kept telling me it is very very normal. Everyone feels this way. Everyone is sometimes attracted to men or women and it is normal. I told her it is not SOMEtimes. I told her it is all the time. She was like. Yeah right! then all other guys your age would do that too. I told her. No ammi they dont. I have lived with guys all my life and I know they dont. She was like you think this way but it isnt so. You are normal. Do not worry.

She again didnt believe that but we went on.

Basically after about 2 hours I think she didnt accept it. She thinks that I have been in bad company that is why I THINK that I am gay. And something happened that started making me think like this. And if I have these emotions then they are normal. Now she only needs to talk to me a whole lot so I can become straight. Well like I said. I dont think I 'came out' right.

Well I think she is denial this will sink is slowly. Thank god. I can deal with that.

Oh and yes about leaving home. Now I am going to start looking for a new place with my mom. So I dont kill myself out of irritation or make their lives miserable as well.

 It sure is hell coming out to someone who is straight and doesnt have any knowledge of the whole being gay thing.

***

Black Fish

20 Oct 2003
02:48 hrs

Well after a long long time I did something useful with my free time. I went to see a stage performance. A comedy stage performance. They are a Comedy Improvisation Troupe. Pakistans first. They are called the 'Black Fish' and their show is called the same thing. Thank God I live in Karachi. The rest of Pakistan is just overgrown villages. But I digress.

Well they were marvellous. They kept the audience involved. They made some GOOD humour out there. They asked the audience for stuff like comments and situations and personality quirks and they were fabulous about it. All in all it was a wonderful show. Sortof something like 'Whose line is anyways'. But live and no cameras so it is much much more real and intense.

And the thing that I left out. The guy who was the compere who was sortof hosting the whole thing and carrying it through is very very attractive. I did see him up close. And WOW ;). I would say he is one of the most sexy men I have EVER seen in my life in person. He was awesome. I was drooling all over the place. And I havent stopped thinking about him since ;). He is one of the very very few people who I would add to the list of people allowed to deflower me ;) and to the list of the 10/10 men. All in all WOW.

Damn! I am still thinking about him continuously. He was so so so 10/10. Ahhhhhhh. But I am sure he is str8. Damn str8 men! ;)

***

20 Oct 2003

Search Engines and Shame
02:57 hrs

Whosoever searched for "watch gay gusy fuck" on netscape.

1 – Shame on you.

To Netscape.

1 – I hate you.

2 – This is a lie and I will not have it on my name.

3 – I hate you.

To myself.

1 – Why do I use such words on my blog.

2 – Why do I feel bad when people stumble across my blog looking for porn but end up cursing me.

3 – I hate Netscape.

***

Filed under Uncategorized

Dream Lover

20 Oct 2003
23:47 hrs

If dreams are at all to be believed. The compere/ commentator/ host guy just ravished me last night. I have never been happier in my life.

***

21 Oct 2003

The Dinner Table Humiliation   00:04 hrs

Me and my friends were at a restaurant. And I was actually humiliated. First everyone. I repeat everyone kept making fun of me for all the time. Then when we went for tea they decided that since Shams isnt reacting to us they threw water at me and called me a sissy infront of everyone. They just did that and laughed like hell at the spectacle that I was in. Wow I am so proud of myself being the the village idiot all through my life. I am so proud of not reacting properly because it might have had a negative effect on the mood of the party. Wow I really am an idiot. Caring about people who dont care about me. Shoot. Seems like I am ready for a relationship.

I have also realized another thing. Make friends only with those people who laugh at your jokes. AND. You laugh at theirs. Hence a common sense of humour. The current group of people I hang out with are NOT like that. They are continuously joking and I do not find even one thing worth smiling for whole evenings. Same goes for me. When I say things that would have killed my friends from college the guys here make fun of it and are shocked by my sense of humour or the lack of it.

Oh shoot. Time to find people who are not bored stiff of my company. Oh wait. They arent bored of me. I am their local idiot to make fun of in public places. Hmmm. Whatever. Time to find new friends.

**

Filed under Uncategorized

Rubai of the Self

21 Oct 2003

00:14 hrs

This is a Rubai (sortof like a Quartrain) that I said today.

woh chanda woh sooraj woh saagar woh basti

woh pal pal simatna woh pal pal bikharna

woh hansti hansati si woh meri hasti

Here is a prosaic translation which is a complete disgrace to the original language. Urdu.

that moon that sun that ocean that city

that slightly small slightly long life of mine

that continuous breaking up that continuous rejoining

that happy and smiling life of mine

***

Filed under Uncategorized

21 Oct 2003

Elections of Desire   12:30 hrs

Well I conducted the Intikhaabat (Elections) for the favourite muscles. Here are the results. The Intikhaabat are over.

Shoulder – 14

Stomach – 2

Buttocks – 4

Chest – 7

Back – 0

Thighs – 6

Tongue – 4

 So I would declare the winner as Shoulders. Who shall now enjoy the title of. Ishq-uz-Zaman. or Love of the time. ;)

 A new poll is up.

***

21 Oct 2003

Recurring Dream, Recurring Longing

12:38 hrs

If dreams are at all to be believed. The compere/ commentator/ host guy just ravished me again last night. He is getting some regular appearances. I hope T is ok with this. Because I would hate it if T came and kicked my butt for being such a slut in my dreams.

***

Filed under Uncategorized

The Turkish Backup

I had a nice chat with one of my friends from college who is now in the US. When I told him how horny and alone I was he told me he has a Turkish guy there for me :). Now I may seem lonely and horny or what not. But I am NOT so desperate that ALL people who know me keep someone as backup for me ;). I am not THAT desperate. At least not yet. (This was all big talk. Do please do keep someone as backup) :)

I am in love with blogging. The whole concept :). Sharing all those stories. Some of which are SO strange. Enjoying everything that I come across(not really everything but just trying to please all of you who WILL read this). I have had some of the most hilarious moments on peoples blogs lately. I have also gotten some good advice through my blog. Thank You.

The compere guy I dream about every night is called Saad Haroon. Why is every Saad sexy? I have no idea but it is a general observation. If I ever have a son he gets named Saad, Fahd, Shams or oh yes something that his other parent wants ;) Who says I am inconsiderate?

Oh and yes there is a friend of mine called Saad. He reads this blog. Saad, I do NOT think you are sexy so calm down. :)

***

Filed under Uncategorized

The Horny Hours

22 Oct 2003
15:56 hrs

I am feeling extremely horny right now. I am seriously deprived of sex. I am beginning to suspect that if I do not have sex VERY soon I will do some irreparable damage to my body. And my soul.

***

Filed under Uncategorized

22 Oct 2003

The Drew Carey Show

17:56 hrs

Yes I will agree that I have an interesting(read strange) sense of humour. One tv show that I love to watch "The Drew Carey Show". Just watched it and I love it.

***

Filed under Uncategorized

23 Oct 2003
Searches and Sorrows
12:57 hrs

What the hell is my site doing in the search results for "begging as a profession in karachi"

Why Allah WHY ?

And for the guy who searched on Yahoo for ... "search for karachi girls her lost the virginity in age 16 to 19"

Dude! what were you thinking ?

***

Filed under Uncategorized

23 Oct 2003

Feast of Desire

13:57 hrs

I just realized. For the first time in my life. I will give up a meal to have sex. Allah, I so need to get laid. It is completely disorienting me.

***

23 Oct 2003
Food and the Homeland
16:03 hrs

I just had an excellent lunch of 'Koftay' (Spicy Meatballs), White Rice and Raita. Followed by a wonderful assortment of fruit. Now I am beginning to think that the Iranian order of eating food i.e Fruit, Food and Sweet is better than what we practice i.e Food, Food, Sweet, Fruit. So from now on I will follow the Iranian method.

Also while eating the fruits is realized one thing. Pakistani fruit are so much better than those in America or Saudi Arabia. When I went to the US I loved to try different things to eat. And the fruit there ... sorry to say were not all that good. And in Saudi Arabia the fruit sucked as hell. The most horrible fruit in the world.

Now Pakistani fruits are very juicy, sweet and have a strong smell. And when I say this I mean it. I found that fruits in America are less juicy, less sweet and do not have the wonderful aroma that makes you hungry all over again. I agree that fuits in America are about 2 times larger than the largest in Pakistan. They are excellent for filling an empty stomach. But Pakistani fruits are the darlings of the gourmand. Thank God Pakistan has something to be proud of. Something that I can fight for and win in the end due to the presence of actual examples. But yes I LOVED the Pears and Peaches in America, Pakistani Pears and Peaches do not come near those.

***

Filed under Uncategorized

23 Oct 2003
Mango Wars
16:08 hrs

A note about Indians and Pakistanis. Basically we are both peace loving people. It is the government that keep us at each other's throats. But despite that there are some things where we are violently against each other. And yes Kashmir isnt one of them. You will never see two people fight over Kashmir.

The things that we will NEVER agree on are

3 – Who has better Men. (DUUUH! Pakistan!)

And to all of you Indians out there. WE HAVE BETTER MANGOES !!! OK !!! YOU LOSE !!!

***

Filed under Uncategorized

23 Oct 2003

Words of Praise

22:40 hrs

I have wonderful news. I am one of the most beautiful men in Pakistan. Says who ? Well if you search Yahoo for "the most beautiful man in pakistan" my blog is listed as No.14. So. YEY.

 And whoever searched for that. Dude! Come over and meet me. And if you are a dudette. Lets go out and hunt for guys ;)

 And whoever searched for "paindabad urdu meaning". Paindabad in Urdu means "Live for Ever"(Common Usage) or "Stay for Ever"(Very Uncommon Usage). And yes I did not have to look up a dictionary as many of you might have thought. I am very well adept in Urdu. Thank you very much.

***

Filed under Uncategorized

23 Oct 2003

The Bus Ride

23:35 hrs

Well after a VERY long time I had an opportunity to travel on a Bus in Karachi. Now I should tell you. You CAN NOT read on it. Because of the horrible AND loud AND cheap music being played on it. And also because the other passengers have to talk and they talk OVER the music. Which pretty much makes it horrible enough for you to start screming and jump out of the bus into the loving embrace of the rear wheels with sweet sweet relief from all that is good and bad about life.

Also Pakistani busses are very beautifully decorated. The whole interior and exterior is painted which arabesques and other patters of animals and flowers and many many traditional patterns. They are horrible to look at closely but the overall effect is wonderful. And generally the patters are very very cheap. But today while I was sitting in the bus I noticed a very interesting pattern. Upon looking closely I saw that it was a very well made and very beautifully designed Mughal Styled Pattern and to be honest it was WONDERFUL. From now on I will always look closely when I am on a bus.

***

Filed under Uncategorized

24 Oct 2003

The Concorde Age

13:39 hrs

Today will the day that the last Concorde landing will take place. This will be a flight from NYC to London. After it the era will end.

When I was very young my father bought me a book about airplanes. The centerfold was a large picture of the Concorde. I remember my father told me about the Concorde and how fast and loud it used to be. I have always been fascinated by the Concorde since then. It was one of my dreams to fly around the world on a Concorde. But well things change. Maybe in the future we will have something better.

But it has to be admitted that it is the end of an era. The Concorde Age.

***

Filed under Uncategorized

24 Oct 2003

Walk on the Footpath   13:41 hrs

Why do people walk on the road when there is a footpath there?

Walk on the damned footpath. What the hell is it there for ?

***

Filed under Uncategorized

25 Oct 2003

Musafir Hoon Yaaron

13:40 hrs

I am currently listening to "musafir houn yaaron na ghar hay na thikana". Yes the old Indian movie song. It is wonderful. The music is complimented by the lyrics and the voice. I love this song. And when I saw the video of this song it fit in with the essence of the song.

"mera jeevan kora kaghaz kora hi reh gaya". We used to make the following parody of this song in university "mera paper kora kaghaz kora hi reh gaya".

***

Filed under Uncategorized

Four Thousand Souls

25 Oct 2003
13:41 hrs

It seems that 4,000 people have been contaminated by my blog. Unfortunate!

And I am looking forward to more of you in the future.

***

Filed under Uncategorized

26 Oct 2003

Family Fatigue   16:49 hrs

I am sorry but this is going to be another post about me and my family.

I am not mentally unstable. I have periods where I am in a bad mood. Doent mean that I am insane. But I hate my life with my family. I cannot get along with my mom at all. I cannot give time to my sisters who feel neglected. I cannot do my work properly due to this. I want the house to be kept properly which my mom can not do and I get very seriously irritated.

Basically I am just a fucking loser. I have failed in practical life. I cannot live like this. I cannot talk to my mom about all this because she has stopped listening to me. I was so irritated with getting luch SO late ... at about 5 pm that I was very rash with my sister. She was crying because of me. When I went to talk to her. She told me that I am a horrible person and that she hates me.

Well that is more like a day in my life. I have constant fights with everyone. Noone else fights with anyone else. I am the animal in the house who fights with everyone. They all say that I am a bad person. They all blame me for it. And I and they all feel that I am a loser, failure and a horrible person.

Wow. I love my life. It is really really nice being like this. I mean why would someone ever NOT want a life where they are have fallen in the eyes of others and in their own eyes as well.

***

Filed under Uncategorized

26 Oct 2003

Overload

17:00 hrs

Too fucking depressed to do anything. I am so afraid that if this keeps up I will have a nervous breakdown. Hurting my family even more.

I can feel that in about half an hour ill need to start blaming someone else but me. Which invariable ends up being Allah. And I will again become seriously blasphemous.

Way to go Shams.

***

Filed under Uncategorized

26 Oct 2003

Embarrased   17:12 hrs

My mom and my sisters told me father that I lock
my door for hours and sit on the Internet. He thinks
I am hooked to porn. I was so embarrased. I want to
die. And honestly it is a lie. I dont sit on the
computer when I lock my door. When my door is
locked. I cry. That is what I am doing. And they lied
to my father about me who now thinks that I am
some sort of a Perverted Maniac.
 Way to go Shams.

***

Breaking Point

26 Oct 2003
18:01 hrs

The breaking point has been reached.

***

Filed under Uncategorized

Two-Faced Mercy

27 Oct 2003

00:52 hrs

I have just realized one thing about myself. I love to care about people. I want to care about people. I would love to sacrifice for people and do something for them and redeem myself.

But I dont.

I am scum. I dont care about people at all although I would love to. Which brings me to the completely two faced attitude towards life.

I am a bad guy who wants to be a good guy but can not because he is a bad guy.

I hate all this. Maybe I am going insane. Maybe I am already insane because no normal human would think the way I do.

FUCK! what if I am insane. What if I think I am normal but I am insane. What then ? Who will tell me ? And if they do tell me do they know what they are talking about?

After reading this post I think ill go find some drug and lose consciousness for 1-2 days so that I can calm down.

***

Filed under Uncategorized

27 Oct 2003

The Irritating Self

00:57 hrs

I am sure people who might be unlunky enough to read my blog regularly would be very very irritated and angry at my posts and the strange content therein.

Honestly. I am as irritated and angry.

***

Filed under Uncategorized

Democracy and Prayer

27 Oct 2003
04:19 hrs

Well I am chatting with a friend on MSN right now. He has the very very special position of actually having a brain.

We were discussing the state of Pakistan trying to be Democratic and Islamic at the same time. Since they are either/ or situation we can be deemed neither. And this is so cute. He said "we cannot be islamic and democratic at the same time .. duhh !!". And I am thinking. WOW. At least there are other people who think like me. THANK GOD!

So we did decide that we cannot be both Democratic and Islamic or for the matter either. We also decided that honour killings are actually sick and perverted and should not take place. I have no idea why the rest of Pakistan doesnt agree with this VERY VERY simple explanation.

I decided that I would rather poke red hot pokers into my brain, through the eyes, than go to offer namaz (prayer) (somewhat like sunday church) on fridays. And I have been dodging it for a LONG LONG time now. THANK ALLAH!

***

Filed under Uncategorized

27 Oct 2003

David Fumero   05:15 hrs

This is more like stating the obvious. But. OH MY GOD!

David Fumero!

OH MY GOD! WOW WOW WOW!

How can someone ever be so so so sexy.

***

The First Sip

27 Oct 2003
13:58 hrs

Ok I know that Alcohol is very strictly Haram or Forbidden in Islam. I also know that it is considered as one of the biggest social evils. But I had to try it once.

Today was chosen as the day when I do it. I was with a friend who had done it before. Since it is illegal to possess or drink alcohol he had to go to people and bring it back with secrecy.

Well we cooled it. It was some sort of a Lager from The Netherlands. Well I opened it up. There was a strange smell. I asked my friend is this normal. He said yes. He asked me if I had ever had Malt. And I said no. Turns out I had only had fruit juices, milk, carbonated drinks and other normal things to drink. He told me not to drink too much at once as I would be repulsed by the taste.

Well I took a small sip. My mouth was filled with a cold cold liquid. Oh so this is what it feels like. Nice. EWWWWW. Suddenly the taste hit me. BITTER! It was BITTER!. I was shocked. What the hell and it has another taste mixed with the bitter. So I asked my friend to check it out because I think it has gone bad. He checks it out to humour me. And then he said "FUCK! It HAS gone bad". And we throw the can away. So now I will have alcohol after the month of Ramazan since the people who can get me the alcohol will not want to anger Allah during the month of Ramazan.

Dont ask. A general level of idioticity in Pakistan regarding Islam and being to obsessed with Islam.

***

Filed under Uncategorized

27 Oct 2003

New Moon

14:48 hrs

All Islamic religious events are according the Islamic calendar. Which is a Lunar rather than a Solar calendar. So every month starts with the sighting of the new moon. Three witnesses have to see the new moon and be witness to the fact. Then it is declared that the moon has been seen and the new month will be from tomorrow.

Due to this the whole muslim world does not have the same even on the same day. At times the dates in the Islamic calendar differ from country to country or even from one town to another.

Every year the people of the North West Frontier Province of Pakistan goes ahead one day from the rest of the country. It was declared that the moon has been sighted yesterday and hence they are all observing the fast of Ramazan today. In the rest of the country that is not so. We will observe fast from tomorrow.

What the hell is this. I am not saying that either they are wrong or we are wrong. I am saying WHAT THE HELL!

***

Filed under Uncategorized

27 Oct 2003

Ramazan Reflections

19:56 hrs

The month of Ramazan is the ninth month of the Islamic calendar. It is considered as the most holy and sacred of months.

Every year. On the 29th and sometimes the 30th of the eighth month. Most muslim families in South Asia climb onto their roofs to look for the new moon. We did that as well. About half an hour before sunset. We wall went on top of the roof. And there we all looked towards the west. The dying glow of the setting sun. Where the new moon will be seen. And yes we saw it. It was a wonderful "pehli ka chaand" or the first days moon. The very light and delicate white curve in the sky.

My family prayed for a good ramazan. And thanked Allah for the beginning of the auspicious month. I was just thinking about the whole concept of religion. Why people believe what they believe? Why are they told to believe? Why do all religions champion the cause of the oppressed but cause oppression on their own.

Well tomorrow will be the first Roza (Fast) of Ramazan. All muslims well be supposed to stay without food, drink and well ;o sex for the duration of daybreak till sunset. I will not keep the Roza. I have never missed any Roza in the last few years as I was very strict in observing the Roza. But not this year.

I love the concept of Sehri(Pre Sunrise Meal). Everyone getting up in the middle of the night. Cooking and eating. Actually feeding like hell since you wont have anything else to eat OR drink till sunset. And I love the specific things that we cook for Sehri that we dont have usually in normal times. Pheeni is one of these things that I love.

Same goes for Aftari(Post Sunset Meal). Everyone ravenously hungry from the Roza. Eating hurriedly but not too hurriedly because the elders kept telling you not to eat fast as it is bad for your health. And then there are all those specific Aftari collection of foods. Fruit Chaat, Dahi Bhallay, Jalaybee etc etc etc. Wow. I am already hungry ;)

**

Filed under Uncategorized

28 Oct 2003

Ramazan Mubarak

19:59 hrs

To all muslims worldwide who will observe the Roza
in the way of Allah.
Ramazan ka chaand mubarak ho.
Congratulations on the new moon of Ramazan.

***

28 Oct 2003

Fuzon Fever   20:51 hrs

I just saw the video of the Group Fuzons new song "Tere bina jiya naheen jaey" (I cant live without you). And well the guy is the video is so hot. I think I am going to have a small heart attack out of an overdose of sheer delight.

***

28 Oct 2003

Google Bafflements

21:34 hrs

I agree that in my time I have conducted some STRANGE searches on google and yahoo. But the following just baffle me. And also the fact that they both led to my blog. Which is again. Shocking.

– "Pakistani parents search Boy for there Daughters"

– "WHAT ARE THE RESPONSIBILITES OF A WAITER"

Now I have NO idea what to say. :)

***

Filed under Uncategorized

29 Oct 2003

Pick Up My Jaw   02:10 hrs

From personal experience. The following line doesnt work the wonders that you expect it to work when you meet a VERY hot guy for the first time.

"Excuse me! can you help me pick up my jaw ... it has fallen on the curb"

I was assuming that he KNEW he was HOT. But whatever. Ill NEVER do that again.

***

29 Oct 2003

Hottest Cities

02:16 hrs

Ok the results are out.

 Question : The hottest men are from … (dont try to be patriotic, be truthful)

Karachi – 8 30%

Istanbul – 2 7%

Sydney – 4 15%

Rome – 2 7%

Paris – 0 0%

Rio de Janeiro – 8 30%

Montreal – 1 4%

***

Filed under Uncategorized

29 Oct 2003

New Vote   02:19 hrs

A new vote is up. And yes ... Intikhaabat means elections.

  If you find a choice not listed in the possible answers leave a comment and I will add it.

*****

29 Oct 2003

First Real Drink   02:23 hrs

Today I actually had some Alcohol properly for the first time in my life. It was a can of "Grolsch Premium Lager" which is from Holland. It has about 5% alcohol.

My comments. Well it had the worst taste of anything to touch my taste buds since I gained the knowledge of my existence. Basically I have to be told that there are good tasting alcoholic beverages because if there arent. Then this was the end for me and alcohol.

***

Filed under Uncategorized

Small Mercies

29 Oct 2003
23:54 hrs

I was just forcibly given a facial by my sisters.
DARN IT! Who am I kidding.
I just forced my sisters into giving me a facial.
I am so gay. ;)

***

Filed under Uncategorized

29 Oct 2003

Desperate Pleasures

23:57 hrs

I just looked at a picture of David Fumero in a policemans uniform and I think I am frothing at the mouth.

I am SO gay.

I just remembered that I have a higher than average IQ.

I am SO SO SO gay. ;)

***

Filed under Uncategorized

A Night for Romance

30 Oct 2003
00:35 hrs

I seem to be in a VERY romantic mood tonight. I mean I want to do something with someone. Like watching some tv. Or a movie. Drinking some nice cold lemonade. With the fan on full. With the whole sensation. The nice warm Karachi breeze coming in the window. I just dont know why but I had a VERY strong sudden urge for this.

I just want to lie in my bed with someone and watch one of those wonderful movies that fell you with a feeling of awe and adventure. One of those movies where you have to sit for a little while after it is over. Where you cannot just move because your whole mood has been changed by the movie.

Like "Legends of the Fall" or "Moulin Rouge". A movie from another age. From another location. Of unbridled adventure and feelings. Something wonderful. With someone. I really want that right now.

Instead I am alone and blogging. I wonder what T is doing right now. I wonder where he is. What he is thinking.

So I think I will go and immerse myself in romantic delusions.

***

Filed under Uncategorized

30 Oct 2003

Argument and Desire

22:12 hrs

Why are SOME people so VERY stupid. Why do they end up mortifying themselves with horrible deeds.

I got into and argument today. With someone who turned out to have a full working brain. Since I am mentally retarded I tend to act strangely. In an argument I will not stop arguing until the other person tells me that I am right and he is wrong.

I told you I am strange!

But today I acted even more strangely that usual. What can be stranger than this? Well read on and ye shall see. EVEN more than usual? Yes.

I got into the argument because I thought the other guy was an idiot. But he turned out to have a brain. Since I was in an argument (Yes I know I am strange.)(YES I KNOW)(FOCUS ON THE DAMNED STORY) I could not back down until he declared I was right and he was wrong.

It turned out like this. He was saying something that I COMPLETELY believe in. Since I AM a buffoon I opposed it. I ended saying the most idiotic things EVER. Until it became painfully obvious to everyone that I WAS wrong and that he WAS right. I would rather jump into a chauldron of rat fat and ox testes than admit that I am wrong in an argument. I told you I am strange. So I just quietned down and the discussion went over to more interesting topics.

The result of this whole thing is.

WANT HIM! I WANT HIS SEED! I wanted to have him right there on the Persian carpet. But alas fate was against me.

***

Filed under Uncategorized

31 Oct 2003

The Old Man and the Izarband

01:17 hrs

I am feeling like utter scum right now. Me and my cousin went to buy some smokes. He went in to the store and I sat in the car. A guy comes up. Very old, white hair and a white beard. He says "izarband khareed lo" (buy these cloth belts) and I say "nahin nahin" (no no). I thought he would leave but he didnt. He said "acchay laga doon ga" (ill give you a good bargain) and I say "nahin nahin". Then he just says "Mushkil kay waqt main kisi ki cheez khareedna bhi sawab ka kaam hay" (in bad times if you buy something from someone even that is a good deed) and he left and went into the bazaar. I was shocked and spellbound. I didnt have a single rupee with me so I couldnt buy anything. But I felt so bad. He was very very poor. He was in a MUCH MUCH bad condition that I was. I kept looking at him until he disappeared in the crowd. What he said to me felt like the breaking of my bond with being a human. I feel like I have betrayed myself.

***

Filed under Uncategorized

**Rubai: The Shattering
and Gathering of Life**

A rubai that I said today.

Kya Shafaq Subha Ki Hay Phooti Kya Hua Ujala
Hay Dekho

Hay Naey Khiyalon Ki Basti Hay Naee Ummeedon
Ka Alam

Yeh Waqt Anokha Hay Samjho Yeh Waqt Nirala
Hay Dekho

Prosaic translation

has the light of day come has the light spread all
over

in the new crop of flowers look at all the new colours
of these faces

it is a city of new thoughts it is a world of new hopes

know that this is a unique time see that this is a rare
time

again apologies for the horrible translation

***

Glossary

A

abbu. Urdu. Father; affectionate form of address.

adhan. Arabic. Call to prayer (also azan/azaan).

allah. Arabic/Urdu. God.

ammi. Urdu. Mother; affectionate form of address.

ashura. Arabic. 10th of Muharram; day of mourning/commemoration.

astaghfirullah. Arabic. "I seek forgiveness from God."

azan. Urdu. Call to prayer (also adhan/azaan).

B

barsaat. Urdu/Hindi. Rainy season; monsoon.

bas. Urdu/Hindi. Enough/that's it.

bazaar. Persian→Urdu. Market.

bazar. Var. of bazaar.

bhai. Urdu/Hindi. Brother; respectful address to a man.

biryani. Urdu. Rice dish with meat/veg and spices.

C

chaand. Urdu/Hindi. Moon; also in Chaand Raat (night before Eid).

chai. Hindi/Urdu. Tea.

chappal. Urdu/Hindi. Slipper/sandal.

clifton. Karachi locality.

D

dargah. Urdu/Persian. Sufi shrine.

defence. Karachi locality (DHA).

dua. Arabic/Urdu. Prayer; supplication.

E

eid. Arabic/Urdu. Islamic festival; Eid al-Fitr, Eid al-Adha.

P

pakora. Urdu/Hindi. Spiced gram-flour fritter.

pir. Urdu/Persian. Sufi guide/elder.

Q

qawwali. Urdu/Persian/Arabic. Sufi devotional music.

qorma. Urdu. Braised curry dish (also korma).

R

raag. Indic. Melodic framework in South Asian classical music (also raga).

raga. Indic (Sanskrit). See raag.

ramadan. Arabic/English form of Ramazan.

ramazan. Urdu. Islamic month of fasting (also Ramadan).

rickshaw. South Asian usage. Three-wheeler auto; common transport.

rishta. Urdu/Hindi. Match/proposal (marriage).

roza. Urdu/Persian. Fast; abstention during Ramazan.

S

saddar. Karachi locality.

salah. Arabic. Formal prayer in Islam (Urdu: namaz).

samosa. Urdu/Hindi. Fried pastry with savory filling.

sehri. Urdu. Pre-dawn meal before the fast (Arabic: suhoor).

shaadi. Urdu/Hindi. Marriage; wedding.

shair. Urdu. A couplet (also sher).

sharif. Urdu/Arabic. Respectable; conforming to social norms.

shayari. Urdu. Poetry/poetic expression.

sher. Urdu. A couplet (also shair).

subhanallah. Arabic. "Glory be to God."

suhoor. Arabic. Pre-dawn meal before the fast (Urdu: sehri).

T

thappar. Urdu/Hindi. Slap.

U

uff. Urdu/Hindi. Exasperation "ugh."

W

wudu. Arabic. Ritual ablution before prayer (Urdu: wuzu).

wuzu. Urdu. Ritual ablution before prayer (Arabic: wudu).

Y

yaar. Urdu/Hindi. Friend; exclamation like "mate/dude."

Z

zikr. Arabic. Remembrance (of God); Sufi devotional practice.

KHAJISTAN

Made in the USA
Middletown, DE
19 November 2025

20814093R00130